The Sales Funnel Book

v2.0

The Simple Plan To Multiply Your
Business With Marketing Automation

Nathan Williams

Copyright

First Printing: 2018

ISBN-13: 978-1719205283

ISBN-10: 1719205280

Crazy Eye Media, LLC

PO Box 2871

Chester, VA 23831

https://www.crazyeyemarketing.com

Disclaimers

Limit of Liability / Disclaimer of Warranty

While the publisher and author have used their best efforts in preparing this book, they make no representations or warranties regarding the accuracy or completeness of the contents of this book. The publisher and author specifically disclaim any implied warranties of merchantability or fitness for a particular purpose, and make no guarantees whatsoever that you will achieve any particular result. Any case studies that are presented herein do not necessarily represent what you should expect to achieve, since business success depends on a variety of factors. We believe all case studies and results presented herein are true and accurate, but we have not audited the results. The advice and strategies contained in the book may not even be suitable for your situation, and you should consult your own advisors as appropriate. The publisher and author shall not be held liable for any loss of profit or any other commercial damages, including but not limited to special, incidental, consequential, or other damages. The fact that an organization or website is referred to in this work as a citation and/or a potential source of information does not mean that the publisher or author endorses the information the organization or website may provide or the recommendations it may make. Further, readers should be aware that Internet websites listed in this work may have changed or disappeared after this work was written.

Earnings Disclaimer

We don't believe in get rich programs – all human progress and accomplishment takes hard work. As stipulated by law, we cannot and do not make any guarantees about your ability to get results or earn any money with your ideas, information, tools, or strategies. After all, it takes hard work to succeed in any type of business. Nothing in this book or any of our websites is a promise or guarantee of results or future earnings, and we do not offer any legal, medical, tax, or other professional advice. Any financial numbers referenced here, or on any of our sites, are simply estimates or projections, and should not be considered exact, actual, or as a promise of potential earnings – all numbers are illustrative only.

Table Of Contents

Preface

In 2012, I left the US Army to start a business as a personal trainer.

I studied hard, took the test, received my personal training certification and was ready for clients!

To get clients, I decided to build a website.

After a couple months, I still had zero clients.

I figured I needed more traffic to my site, so I Google'd "how to get traffic".

Long story short, this set me off on the path to becoming a digital marketing entrepreneur!

Within a year, I had closed down my personal training business to focus on digital marketing full time.

A few months later, I was making pretty good money as an affiliate marketer. Not "F-you money", but enough that my wife and I weren't worried.

I had all sorts of crazy link pyramids and wheels. I had a Private Blog Network (PBN). I had $1,000+ tools that would spin articles and auto post them across the web. I was running a couple Virtual Private Servers (VPS) 24/7 to help me build links...

All this in an effort to rank #1 on Google so people would visit my site, click on my affiliate link, and I'd earn a commission.

As I said, it was working well, until one day, Google launched an algorithm update called Penguin which essentially wiped my "business" off the face of the planet overnight.

I quickly cascaded into a downward spiral, trying everything I could to get back what I had lost.

Nothing worked.

Ultimately, I got a 9-5 job and had to pursue my digital marketing career on the side...

However, this time, I took a different approach.

I wasn't trying to "game" the system.

I wasn't trying to "get rich quick".

I was going to build an actual business.

Something sustainable.

Eventually, I got into list building. Then paid traffic. Then funnels and automated sales systems.

I began piecing all these various elements together into a strategy I call the **Interest Driven Sales Funnel**.

It's a funnel/business model that automatically gauges your audience's interests, so you can better relate and sell more.

After figuring all of this out, I was able to quit my 9-5 and get back to running my own business full time.

I've since built dozens of successful Interest Driven Sales Funnels in many niches, offering many products (physical & digital) and services (cheap to high-end)...

And, as you will soon see, this strategy can be applied to ANY business, both online and offline!

I'm really proud and passionate about this strategy because I know it works, I hope you enjoy this book!

Intro

This isn't a book simply about sales funnels, rather it uncovers a business growth strategy **all** businesses can take advantage of.

This strategy can be applied to any business model:

- Ecommerce stores
- Info/digital product sellers
- Coaches & consultants
- Service-based businesses
- Brick & mortar stores
- SaaS
- Affiliate marketers
- Network marketers
- And everything in-between

Within the pages of this book, you will learn how to develop a machine that automatically segments your audience based on their interests, allowing you to better relate to their needs, and giving you the power to sell more!

Exciting stuff, right?!

Also, even though you may think you could just skip down to the Micro Sales funnel you need at the moment, I recommend first reading the entire book from start to finish, because if you don't understand the Macro Sales funnel, your Micro Sales Funnels will never be the best they can be.

Finally, don't skip the annexes. There are some strategies, tactics, and concepts that can help take your understanding to a whole new level.

Without further ado, let's just get into it!

What Is A Sales Funnel?

If you ask 10 people what a sales funnel is, you'll get 10 different answers.

To help alleviate any confusion, I want to give you the explanation we'll use throughout this book.

First, there are two levels of sales funnels:

1. Macro
2. Micro

Macro Sales Funnels

A Macro sales funnel is essentially the "**customer journey**".

Depending on what customer journey model you look at, a customer typically journeys through 4-6 phases:

1. Awareness: of pain, of need, of solution, of your business
2. Interest: they start conducting research
3. Evaluation: they're going to buy something, but they want to make sure they get the "best" one
4. Decision: they buy
5. Retention: keep them happy, sell more
6. Advocacy: they tell everyone about your business

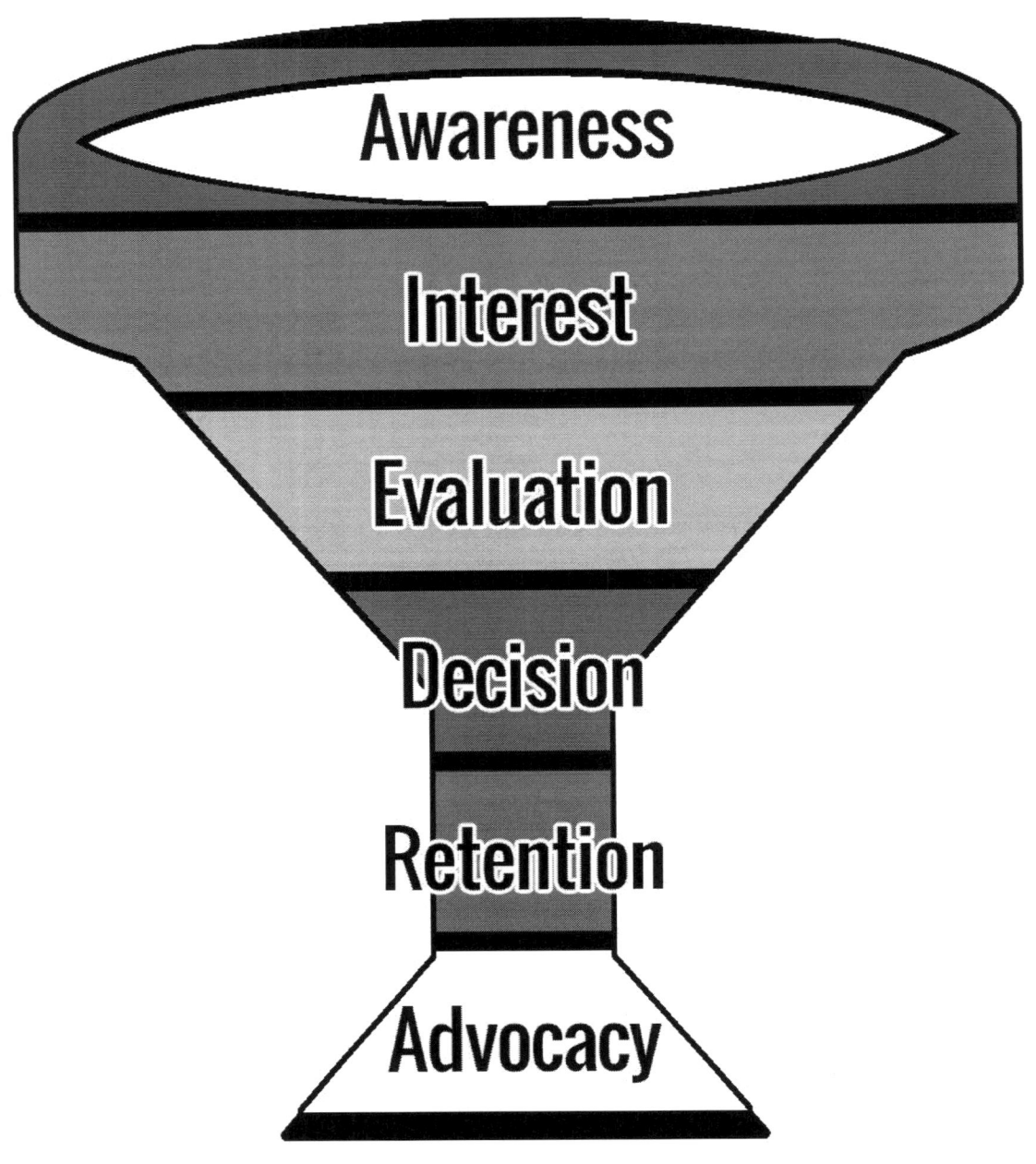

Micro Sales Funnels

A Micro sales funnel contains the actual content, pages, ads, images, videos, automations, emails, messages, phone calls, etc. **used to sell a particular offer** (product/service).

Micro sales funnels are "inside" the Macro sales funnel. They're what actually *move* the customer through their journey.

We will uncover a bunch of Micro sales funnel models in this book; however, here's an example so you have an idea of what I'm talking about:

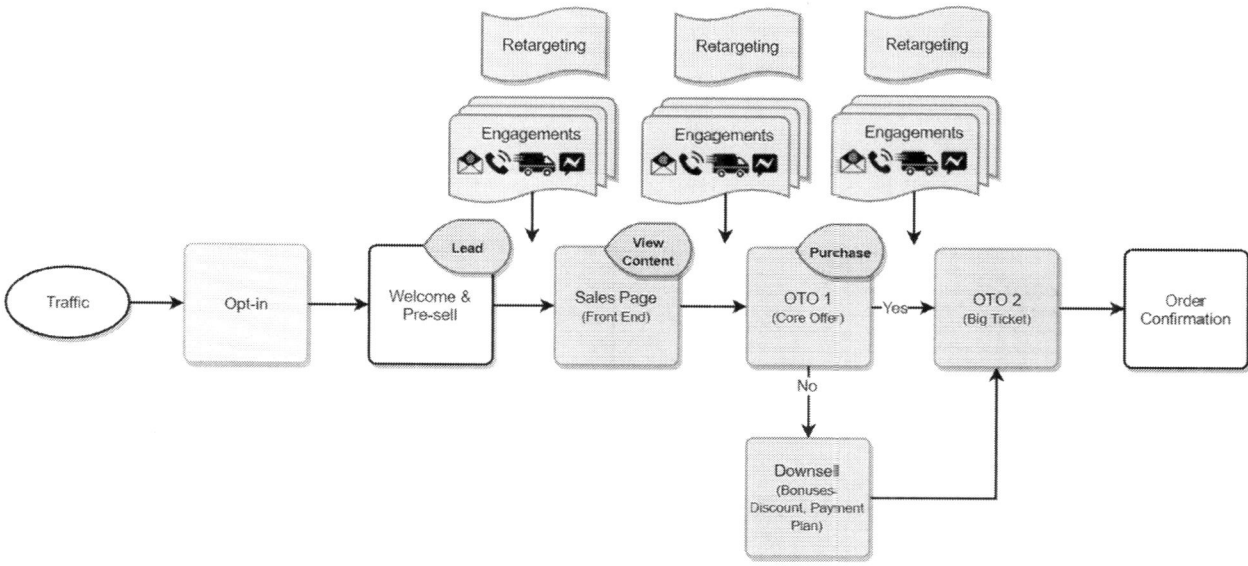

Quick Recap

To quickly summarize, there are two sales funnel levels. There's the Macro sales funnel which your customers journey through, and then there are many Micro sales funnels that sell your products and services and make the customer journey possible.

Interest Driven Sales Funnel Strategy

The Interest Driven Sales Funnel Strategy incorporates both the Macro and Micro levels into one succinct strategy.

Following this strategy will help you build a funnel that automatically molds to your audience's interests, so you can better relate and sell more!

How does it work?

For starters, put content in front of your audience to gain awareness and see how they react. We call this the "Main Series" and we'll go into more detail on it in the next section.

Speaking of audience, I'm referring to your ideal customer (demographics, behaviors, interests, locations, etc.). Maybe they know who you are already, maybe not. Maybe they're on a list already, maybe not. Basically anyone who might buy something from you is included in your audience.

Now, when someone reacts to a piece of your content, they'll be placed (oftentimes, automatically) on a list and in a segment as having shown interest in a particular topic, category, product, service, etc.

You then target people on these lists and in these segments to move them into one (or more) of your various Micro sales funnels that are designed to sell a product/service they're interested in.

After going through one (or more) of your Micro sales funnels, the individual goes back into the Main Series so you can gauge more interest and the cycle repeats itself.

Huge Benefits

The first benefit of the Interest Driven Sales Funnel is that it allows your audience to **self-segment**.

You don't have to place individuals into different segments you "think" are right. Instead, you *know* what segments people need to be in because they put themselves into the appropriate segment(s) based on their actions.

Picture your funnel (marketing efforts) "adapting" to each individual audience member. It automatically figures out what they like and proceeds to only show them what they want to see.

The second massive benefit of the Interest Driven Sales Funnel is that it's **modular** (plug & play).

This means each Micro Sales Funnel can be plugged in wherever, whenever.

For example, let's say you're launching a new product and you want to build out a Product Launch Micro Sales Funnel. You simply build that funnel, run your audience through it, and end it by returning them to the Main Series where more interests can be identified and more products sold.

This also means it will grow with your business. As you add new products and services to your line with their corresponding Micro Sales Funnels, they plug right into your existing Interest Driven Sales Funnel.

It will grow and expand as you grow and expand.

Ultimately, this makes it incredibly flexible and doesn't bind you in any way.

The third massive benefit of the Interest Driven Sales Funnel is that it's **timeless**. Meaning, it's not dependent upon a certain piece of technology working a certain way.

I'm doing my best to make the majority of this book timeless so whether you pick it up in 2018, when it's written, or 2028, you'll still glean a tremendous amount of value.

Having said that, in most of the later examples, I'll primarily reference email marketing and automation.

While email marketing is far from dying, it will someday.

The good news is, there will always be a way to reach out and engage your audience:

- Email
- Direct Mail
- Text
- Phone
- Ads & Retargeting
- In Person Visits
- Commercials
- Facebook Messenger
- Whatever method the future holds!

The strategy and concepts you're learning in this book will ring true far into the future.

Examples

To illustrate the Interest Driven Sales Funnel, here are a couple **timeless** examples.

Old Folks

Let's pretend we sell products that improve the quality of life for old folks.

I'm talking about 75+ years old, living in assisted living communities, where anything that makes their life a tad easier is greatly appreciated.

We can't really email, text, or run online ads to these folks because this demographic doesn't typically use computers or cell phones.

So, we'll settle with direct mail and phone calls.

We acquire a list of 10,000 old folks' addresses and begin our Main Series (interest gauging content) by sending a postcard about our $100 chair riser with the call-to-action (CTA) to give us a call if they want one.

If someone calls, great! They enter into the Micro Sales Funnel that presents several cross-sells.

Our sales rep takes the order for the chair riser, then recommends a $20 E-Z Reacher, a $30 chair attachment to help them stand, and a $150 heated massage pad to ease pain.

After these offers, the customer goes back into our Main Series where they'll be shown more content and offers so we can gauge interest.

If the individual doesn't call from the first postcard, we send a letter with a customer's success story. It talks about their life before and after the chair riser: how much easier it is to get out of their chair and how their knees feel much better.

The CTA of the letter will again be to give us a call. Of course, our sales rep will take the order and offer the cross-sells of our Micro Sales Funnel.

If the individual doesn't call from our success story letter, we send a postcard for free chair riser blocks. These free chair riser blocks are nowhere near as good as our $100 chair riser; however, they pique interest and get the individual on the phone, where we can up-sell our nice riser plus all the cross-sells.

If all three mailings for our chair riser fall short, it's no problem. Maybe that person doesn't have trouble getting out of their chair.

They're not interested.

Mailing 4 will recommend another product that solves a completely different problem and so on.

Makes sense, right?

Do you see how it's all pre-planned and thought out?

We send 3 pieces of direct mail about one product that solves a particular problem. If the person calls (shows interest), our sales rep takes them through a pre-established cross-sell series of complementary products we know sell well.

Whether they buy our product or not, they return to the Main Series where they're shown other offers that solve entirely different problems. Of course, these offers all have their own Micro Sales Funnels as well with up-sells, down-sells, and cross-sells.

McDonalds

McDonalds does a lot of advertising; however, for this example, I'm only talking about TV ads.

Let's say, for their Main Series (interest gauging content), every three months they launch a TV commercial featuring a new product.

The first new product they launch is an ice cream sundae. You don't really like ice cream, so you ignore it. (no interest)

The next product they launch is the McRib!

"Woo!" You say to yourself, "I'm going to McDonalds!" (interest shown)

You show up at the register, ask for a McRib when they hit you with, "Would you like fries with that?"

Of course you do and a drink to wash it down.

You might as well super-size it, you don't want to be hungry in a few hours.

And, even though you don't really like ice cream, they do have that new sundae; since you're already there, you might as well add it to your order.

Finally, you donate your change to charity.

Before you realize it, instead of spending $4 on a sandwich, you've spent $20 on a meal.

You go back home, feeling nauseous because you shouldn't eat that much McDonalds ever, and wait until another piece of Main Series content resonates with you.

Quick Recap

The Interest Driven Sales Funnel is an all-in-one strategy that incorporates both the Macro and Micro level sales funnels.

To define Interest Driven Sales Funnel in one sentence: You put content in front of your audience, see if they're interested in it, try to sell them stuff they're interested in, and then try to sell them even more stuff they're interested in.

The primary benefits are that it allows your audience to self-segment, it's modular (plug & play), and it's timeless.

The Main Series

I've mentioned the Main Series quite a bit already, now it's time to actually learn what it is and how it works.

The Main Series is the backbone of your Interest Driven Sales Funnel.

It's responsible for **building and maintaining the relationship** with your audience while *simultaneously* **spreading <u>awareness</u>** and **gauging <u>interest</u>**.

It covers the top 2 levels of the Macro level sales funnel.

The Main Series works by engaging with your audience from many **sources**, **mediums**, and **angles** *(more on these in just a second)*. Basically, you're going to put content in front of your audience and "watch" them react to it.

<u>This is important!</u> When I say content, I mean <u>ANYTHING</u> you produce that your audience sees. This includes, but is not limited to:

- Blog Posts
- Videos and Images
- Emails
- Facebook Messenger Messages
- Podcasts
- Ads – *Yes, these are content!*
- Sales Pages – *Also content!*
- Direct Mail
- Phone Calls
- TV Commercials
- Newspaper and Magazine Articles

Like I said, any way for you to spread your message in a way that *reaches your audience*, counts.

Reaching your audience is the most important aspect. There are always new fandangled ways to put your content in front of people. Some sound really cool and you may want to try them out, only to find your audience isn't actually on that platform.

For instance, a few years back I took a training on Pinterest marketing. There were promises of cheap, high quality traffic. Low and behold, the audience I was trying to reach (22-34 year old males) weren't on Pinterest. It didn't matter how technically well I performed my marketing, it was never going to work!

Point being, **you need to promote your content where your audience hangs out**. (don't go after "cheap" traffic just because it's cheap. Focus on the traffic that matters.)

Sources, Mediums, and Angles

There are hundreds of ways to promote your content to your audience. (remember, your audience includes people that don't know you AND people that know you and are on your various lists [retargeting, email, phone, address, etc.]).

The best way to think about your content promotion is by categorizing it based upon sources, mediums, and angles.

- The **Source** is where the traffic comes from, ie. Facebook, Google, ActiveCampaign, Twitter, Instagram, iTunes, New York Times Newspaper, etc.
- The **Medium** is the general category of the Source, ie. Organic ("free"), Cost Per Click (CPC) ("paid"), Email, Facebook Messenger, Phone, Referral, Affiliate, etc.

- The **Angle** is how you present the piece of content to your audience. For example, if your piece of content is about weight loss, you could approach it from the angle of "get your beach body back", or "reduce your risk of heart disease and Type II Diabetes", or "be able to keep up with your kids", or a myriad of other angles. They're all benefits of weight loss, but some resonate better than others depending on your audience, so you need to test them out.

Back on topic...

You're going to put content in front of your audience through various sources, mediums, and angles. We will call this content, Content "Chunks".

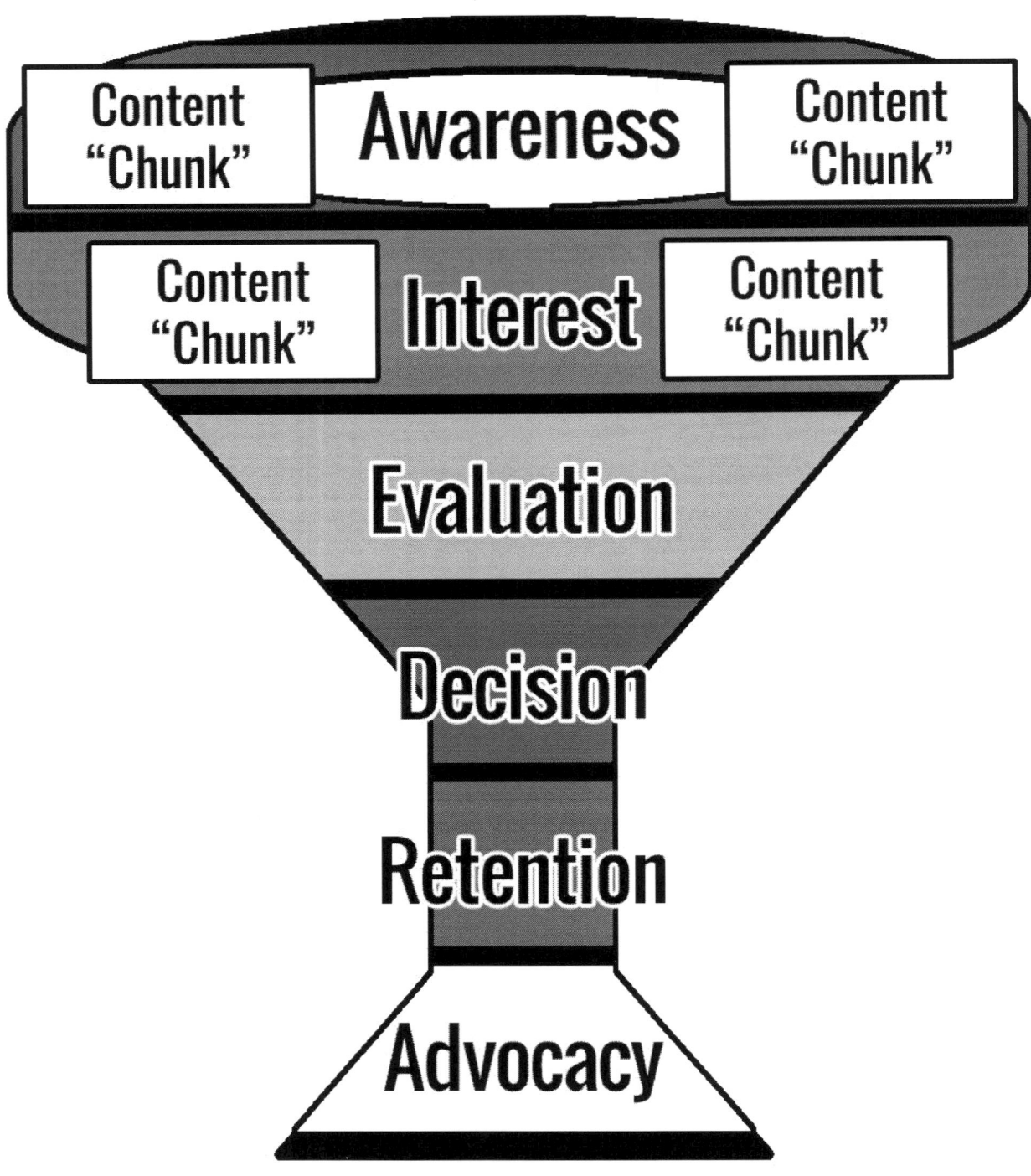

To illustrate the content chunks, let's look at Crazy Eye Marketing. We have the following chunks:

- Facebook Ads
- Marketing Automation

- Sales Funnels
- Digital Marketing Strategy

So, four "chunks" that contain ads, blog posts, videos, podcasts, etc.

We then place those content chunks in front of our audience and whenever an individual shows interest in a piece of content, we add the individual to a list and segment as "interested in whatever 'chunk'" and begin to promote our corresponding Micro Sales Funnel(s)!

Ie. We post an ad on Facebook that links to an article about Facebook Ads. When someone clicks on the ad and lands on the article, they're automatically added to our retargeting list and placed in the "Interested in Facebook Ads" segment. Now, we promote our Micro Sales Funnel that sells our Facebook Ads course.

Interest

To better clarify how we can judge if someone is interested in a topic, product, service, offer, etc. here's a list of ways to gauge interest:

- Click – Someone clicks a link in one of your emails or ads, showing they're interested in a certain topic, offer, etc.
- Pageview – When someone looks at a specific page on your website, it shows they're interested in a certain topic, offer, etc.
  - Multi-pageview – When one view isn't enough, you can "count" the views an individual makes. When they view a specific topic or offer 2+ times, you know they're interested. (this is similar to "points" down below)
- Purchase – When an individual purchases a product or service from you, it's a dead giveaway they're interested in a certain topic, offer, etc.
- Specific Lead Magnet – When someone opts-in to receive a Lead magnet for something related to what you want to sell. For

example, a mini-guide called "5 ways we decreased Facebook Ad spending by 89%" – we know they're interested in Facebook Ads.

- **Phone Call / Reply** – If someone calls in or replies to one of your emails, depending on the reasoning, it could certainly show interest in a particular topic, offer, etc.
- **Survey** – Similar to a phone call or reply in that someone is explicitly telling you what they're interested in.
- **Points (CRM)** – More "advanced"; however, if you're using a CRM tool you can use points to gauge interest and add people to lists and segments based on points. For example, if someone looks at your sales page 5 times, you know they're highly interested and may just need a tad more persuasion - exactly what a Micro Sales Funnel will provide.

As you can see, there are many ways we can gauge interest and; therefore, place them on various lists and in different segments, so we can begin to promote our Micro Sales Funnels.

Add Them To Lists & Segments

When you hear the word "list", what do you think of?

Do you think only of email lists?

That's what I used to think too, until I realized there are many types of lists.

There are:

- Email lists
- Phone/Text lists
- Address lists
- Messenger lists
- *Retargeting lists*

And probably a few more that I'm not thinking of, or that don't exist yet.

For our purposes, **a list is a group of people, whose contact info we have** *(even if it's just from a retargeting pixel)*, **that we can reach out to whenever we want.**

Retargeting Lists

Some lists are easier to add people to than others. For instance, to add someone to a retargeting list, all a person has to do is visit a page on your site, or watch a few seconds of a video on Facebook or YouTube. They don't have to enter any information, they simply have to engage with your content.

The downside of a retargeting list is that you're going to have to pay to put your message in front of your list members. Whereas with a more "traditional" list (email, phone, address, messenger), you can contact individuals as often as you'd like for free or nearly free (of course, you will need to pay for the service and postage if sending physical mail, but it's often cheaper than reaching out to your retargeting lists).

So, a retargeting list can be a bit more expensive to maintain than a traditional email, phone, address, or messenger list, but it's much easier to grow and incredibly powerful.

Segments

Each list will contain various segments. These segments can be broken into:

- Demographics – gender, age, race, job title, education, relationship
- Behaviors – purchases, events, travel
- **Interests** – topics and offers they've shown interest in

The interest-based segments are the most important. It doesn't matter if they're male or female, young or old, buyer or non-buyer... if they don't care about what we're talking about, it doesn't matter.

With that said, knowing the demographics and behaviors can help with your angles. For instance, if you're selling a weight loss product and you're targeting middle-aged men with families, your angle is going to be much different than if you're targeting a young, single female.

Quick Recap

We have a bunch of content we're placing on various sources and mediums - wherever our audience is so we can gauge interest. When interest in a particular topic or offer is shown, we're placing the person on a list or multiple lists and segments. Once they're on a list and in a segment, we will begin to promote our Micro Sales Funnels.

Main Series Patterns

Now that you know the purpose of the Main Series is to **build and maintain the relationship** with your audience while *simultaneously* **spreading <u>awareness</u>** and **gauging <u>interests</u>**, in order to add them to lists and segments...

And while you can theoretically "wing" the content and structure of your Main Series because each piece of content can stand on its own, it's probably not the best strategy.

It's generally best to follow a content pattern or plan for a few reasons:

1. It's more logical for your audience and they'll know what to expect
2. It gives your audience more chances to show interest in a particular topic or offer. Not everyone will act on the first piece of content you put in front of them and by presenting your message

several times, in several different ways, you give your audience more opportunities to act

3. It's easier for you to create content because you know what your next piece should be about

For instance, if you read the "Old Folks" example on page 10, three pieces of content about the same chair riser were sent in a row. Hopefully they showed interest by giving us a call. If not, the fourth piece of content we sent them was for a different offer. This way, we're keeping things fresh!

In this section I'll give you several patterns to help you structure your Main Series.

Just remember, the main goal of the Main Series is to gauge interest! This way you are able to send more relevant information to your audience and sell more via your Micro Sales Funnels.

The 3 Es

Don't be mad, I know I just made a few points on why you should follow a pattern, but this first "pattern" isn't really a pattern at all.

Instead, it's more a way to think about the content you promote.

Each piece of content you promote should have one of these Es as its primary goal:

- **Entertain**: This content is meant to entertain. Videos, pictures, stories, etc. provide great entertainment.
- **Educate**: Helpful content that solves problems, answers questions, and provides guidance. How-to tutorials, white papers, case studies, etc. provide great educational material.

- **Earn**: This content is what generates sales. Sales pages, coupons, discounts, bonuses, etc. provide extra incentive to make a purchase.

While each piece of content should have one clear goal or objective (Entertain, Educate, Earn), they don't have to be mutually exclusive.

For example, if you promote a how-to video, it should definitely be educational, but why not make it entertaining and include a CTA to buy something at the end?

When To Use

You may want to use the 3 E content if you offer TONS of products and services in an incredibly wide variety of categories.

Basically, you should follow this "pattern" when you offer so much "stuff" for a wide variety of interests and you have no idea what your audience member may be interested in.

For example, if you run a massive ecommerce store (250+ products with 10+ unique product categories) and you have 10 top selling products you really want people to see, you may not want to spend a full week promoting each one. It would take 10 weeks for them to see everything you offer.

Instead, you could promote a different offer/product every day. This way, the audience member will see what you offer much sooner and hopefully show interest in a product or two which will launch them into a Micro Sales Funnel.

How To Use: Sources, Mediums, and Angles

3 E content is very versatile and can stand on its own (the audience member doesn't need to read/watch/listen to the previous piece of

content to understand the new piece of content). Each piece of content is its own entity.

With that said, depending on the source, medium, and angle you present your content, the frequency in which you promote your content will change.

Here are some "standard" frequencies:

- Email: 3-7 per week
- Phone Calls & Text Messages: 1 per week or every other week
- Physical Mail: 1-2 per week
- Facebook: 1-2 per day
- Facebook Messenger: 1-2 per week
- Twitter: 5-15 per day
- Pinterest: 3-11 per day
- LinkedIn: 1 per day
- Instagram: 1-2 per day

Some frequencies pulled from this study by CoSchedule: https://coschedule.com/blog/how-often-to-post-on-social-media/

Of course, if your medium is organic search (SEO) or referral traffic, you probably won't be able to control how it comes in and who clicks what. This is OK. You are still able to add them to retargeting lists and segment them based upon the content they land on.

Closing

Again, this 3 E content isn't so much a pattern as it's a way to think about what you're promoting.

Remember, while each piece of content should have a main objective (entertain, educate, earn), it doesn't mean it can't do all three!

Weekly "Pushes"

I call this pattern "Weekly Pushes" because every week you're trying to sell (push) a different product or service to your audience.

Instead of making random offers or promoting random content depending on your mood, you spend an entire week on the same topic.

This gives people more opportunity to see what you're offering and act, while not being overbearing and "burning" them out.

The Weekly "Pushes" Framework

The goal of this framework is to see if the person is interested in what you're promoting (revisit page 18 for the various ways you can gauge interest).

For the sake of example, I'm going to outline a "push" using email as the medium.

Step 1: Pick a widget to sell.

Step 2: Follow the pattern below for that single widget.

- **Pattern**: 3 and 2 (M, T, W, F, S)

Send 4 to 5 emails on the same topic, for the same offer, during each "push". In general, it's good to break up these emails to give people a little time to react, rather than bombarding them every day. For this reason, I recommend sending 3 daily emails, take a day off, send 2 more daily emails, take a day off, and then repeat with a new "push".

- **Email 1**: Fun/personal story
  - Relate to widget
  - P.S. goes to sales page

People connect with stories. People enjoy stories. We want people to connect with us and enjoy hearing from us, which is why we must share a story! Now, it doesn't necessarily have to be a personal story; you can share a success story from a client or customer or even a well-known individual, like a celebrity, just shared in a different light.

At the end of the story, close out (soft sell) with a simple PS line that takes them to the sales page where they can learn more, if they wish.

- **Email 2**: Promotion of widget
    - Use a marketing formula: Problem-Agitate-Solve, Feature-Benefits-Advantages, Before-After-Bridge (page 52)
    - CTA goes directly to the sales page – "Click Here To Buy"

While stories are great and help us connect, sometimes a good old-fashioned sales letter converts best… especially when they have the story from the previous email rolling around in their head! In this 2nd email, pitch your offer. You can use a marketing formula to help structure your message or just do whatever you think is best.

The call-to-action should be straight forward and to the point with no mystery behind it, "If you're interested in this offer, click here". (How much more "interest gauging" can you get?! If the person clicks that link, we know they're interested in our offer and they'll enter one of our Micro Sales Funnels).

- **Emails 3-4:** Content on topic of offer
    - Link to a blog post that's entertaining and/or educational
    - Include CTAs in both the PS line of the email and within the article itself which link to your offer's sales page

After sharing a story and a "hard" pitch, it's time to ease back a little bit and just share some more information with them. Send links to articles, videos, and other resources they'll find helpful, interesting, and entertaining on the same topic as the offer you're trying to sell.

Include links to your offer's sales page in your email P.S. line and throughout the particular article so they can easily navigate to the sales page, if they're interested in learning more.

- **Email 5**: Content OR Promotion (discount)

Email 5 is optional. If the individual hasn't visited your sales page after 4 emails on the same topic for the same offer... they may simply not be interested in that offer. So, use some discretion here. If you feel like this 5th email is "too much", don't use it.

If you do use Email 5, you can send another piece of content like emails 3 & 4 OR you can make a last-ditch effort to sell your offer by sending another "hard" sales email and/or by offering a bonus or discount.

That completes the Weekly "Pushes" framework! Rinse and repeat with a new product the following week!

Story-Based Series

Story-Based Series are similar to the Weekly "Pushes" in that you're promoting more than one piece of content on the same product/service/topic. However, they're different in that all of your content pieces are "connected".

What do I mean by "connected"?

Think about a TV series like Game of Thrones, Orange is the New Black, The Walking Dead, The Sopranos, Breaking Bad... *hopefully you've watched a TV series before.*

The point is, what do all of these series have in common?

You need to watch all the episodes, in order, to truly enjoy it... but, once you're "in", you're in and likely end up binge watching the whole series!

How do they suck you in and keep you watching?

Cliffhangers.

Or, as us marketers call them, **opening and closing loops**.

As you're watching a TV series, they introduce five different story lines in one episode, but they don't finish any of them in that episode. Instead, they make you wait until the next episode to see what happens; then, they close two of the previously established story lines... and start four more!

It's never ending. As soon as one story line ends, two more start – keeping you hooked.

The idea of opening and closing loops is the core concept behind a Story-Based Series.

How To Use It

In this example, we're going to reference email as our medium; however, the concept applies to any medium that allows you to "drip" content to people.

As I previously stated, send several emails on the same product/service/topic – anywhere from 2 to 10, depending on what you have to share.

As people get sucked into your story and start clicking on links and visiting pages, their actions trigger different Micro Sales Funnels.

Here are a few simple phrases that can be used to open loops:

- More on that later
- You'll find out tomorrow
- In the next email you'll receive X, so be on the lookout for it!

Finally, my last remaining tip is to write all these emails at once. Pick your story, map it out, where are you going to take people, what do you want them to click, how are you going to carry the story across several days. Then, write all 2-10 emails in one go.

These emails can be a rough draft at first, you simply want to make sure you're opening and closing loops in a way that sucks people in.

If you write your emails in multiple sessions, you'll forget which loops you opened and closed and it won't work.

Autoresponder Madness

A fellow by the name of Andre Chaperon is the grandfather of Story-Based Series (he calls them Soap Opera Sequences).

He put together a course called Autoresponder Madness that teaches how to write these Story-Based Series.

It's a solid course and I highly recommend it, if this concept sounds interesting to you!

The course sales page: http://autorespondermadness.com

"Long" Course

The "Long" Course is the pattern I've been using with Crazy Eye Marketing for about three years.

Think of it as if you're teaching your subscriber something long and complex. Consider every piece of content you promote, a lesson.

In my case, I teach the sales funnel concept by taking people through the sections they need to focus on, based on their order of importance and significance.

Of course, along the way, I dribble in different products and services I offer that make sales funnel development easier for my audience.

When To Use It

The "Long" Course model won't fit every type of business; however, it works very well for businesses that offer courses/training/coaching and other services. You teach through the series and it makes a natural transition into selling a course, training, or coaching.

You also want to be able to provide a "linear" path for success - there's Point A and Point B with clear steps to successfully get from Point A to Point B.

Back to my sales funnel "Long" Course example, the path for all sales funnels is the same: customers, business, delivery, the "meat", emails, traffic, etc.

It's a logical path to get from Point A to Point B.

Another example, weight loss: mindset ➔ diets (simple to complex) ➔ exercising (walk, run, first 5k) ➔ supplements, etc.

This is another linear path from Point A to Point B. Of course, many people who are trying to lose weight jump straight to supplements and diet pills; however, the right way is to follow the "Long" course described above.

Example

I think the best way to describe the "Long" Course pattern is by providing an example. Picture it like this:

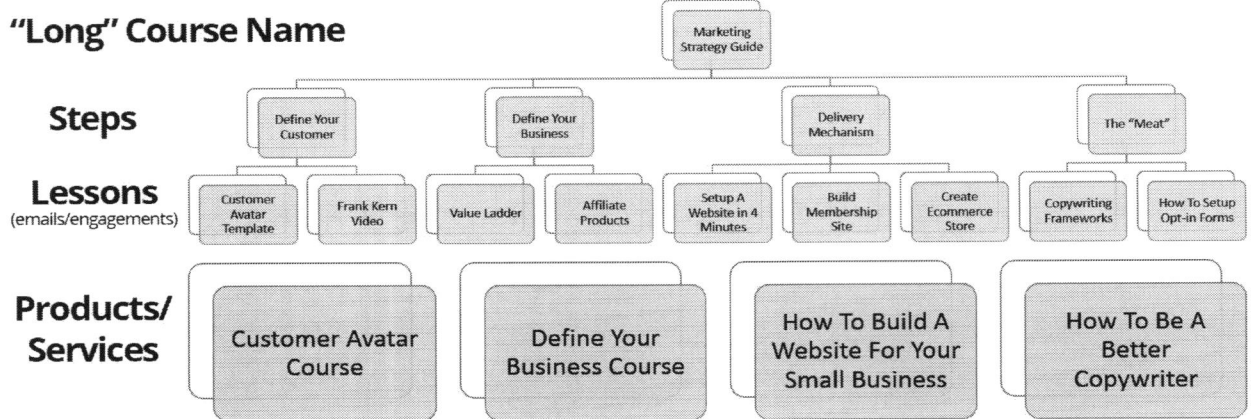

- **"Long" Course Name**: You should give it a name!
- **Steps**: How to get from Point A to Point B
- **Lessons (content)**: The particular blog posts, videos, podcasts, etc. you will promote to your audience to teach them something about the particular step they're on
- **Products/Services**: The corresponding products/service you offer as they relate to each step and/or lesson

As you can see, the "Long" Course is simply your content (blog posts, videos, white papers, reports, etc.) presented in an order that takes an individual from Point A to Point B.

Again, if you offer courses, training, coaching, or services – this pattern can be very effective!

Combining Patterns

I briefly want to address the fact the aforementioned Main Series patterns can certainly be combined.

For example, the majority of my Main Series for Crazy Eye Marketing is a long course. It works very well for what I offer and the market I serve. However, there are segments of it that are more 3 E styled and other segments that are Weekly "Pushes".

Remember, **the point of the Main Series is to gauge interest** while building and maintaining a relationship.

You know your audience better than anyone else, if you think one pattern will work for one product and another pattern for another – mix it up! Or, better yet, split test to see which pattern performs best!

Quick Recap

The Main Series contains a bunch of content and you need to get that content in front of your audience by placing it in various sources and mediums. You then wait for someone to show interest in a piece of your content so you can add them to a list and segment so you can begin promoting Micro Sales Funnels that sell products and services they're most likely interested in. Finally, it's best to follow a pattern or use some strategy behind the content you're sharing in your Main Series because it will help you stay focused and give your audience more chances to show you what they're interested in.

Micro Sales Funnels

As previously mentioned, Micro Sales Funnels contain the actual content, pages, ads, images, videos, automations, emails, messages, letters, phone calls, etc. used to sell a particular offer (product/service).

Quick Note: Every guru has their own "magic" sales funnel they promote, which is cool – check them out. In this section I'm going to cover the foundational funnels. Once you have a solid foundation, you will be able to pick and choose different elements in order to build the best Micro Sales Funnel for your particular business, offer, and audience.

Micro sales funnels are "inside" the Macro sales funnel. They're what actually *move* the customer through their journey and are responsible for selling your products and services.

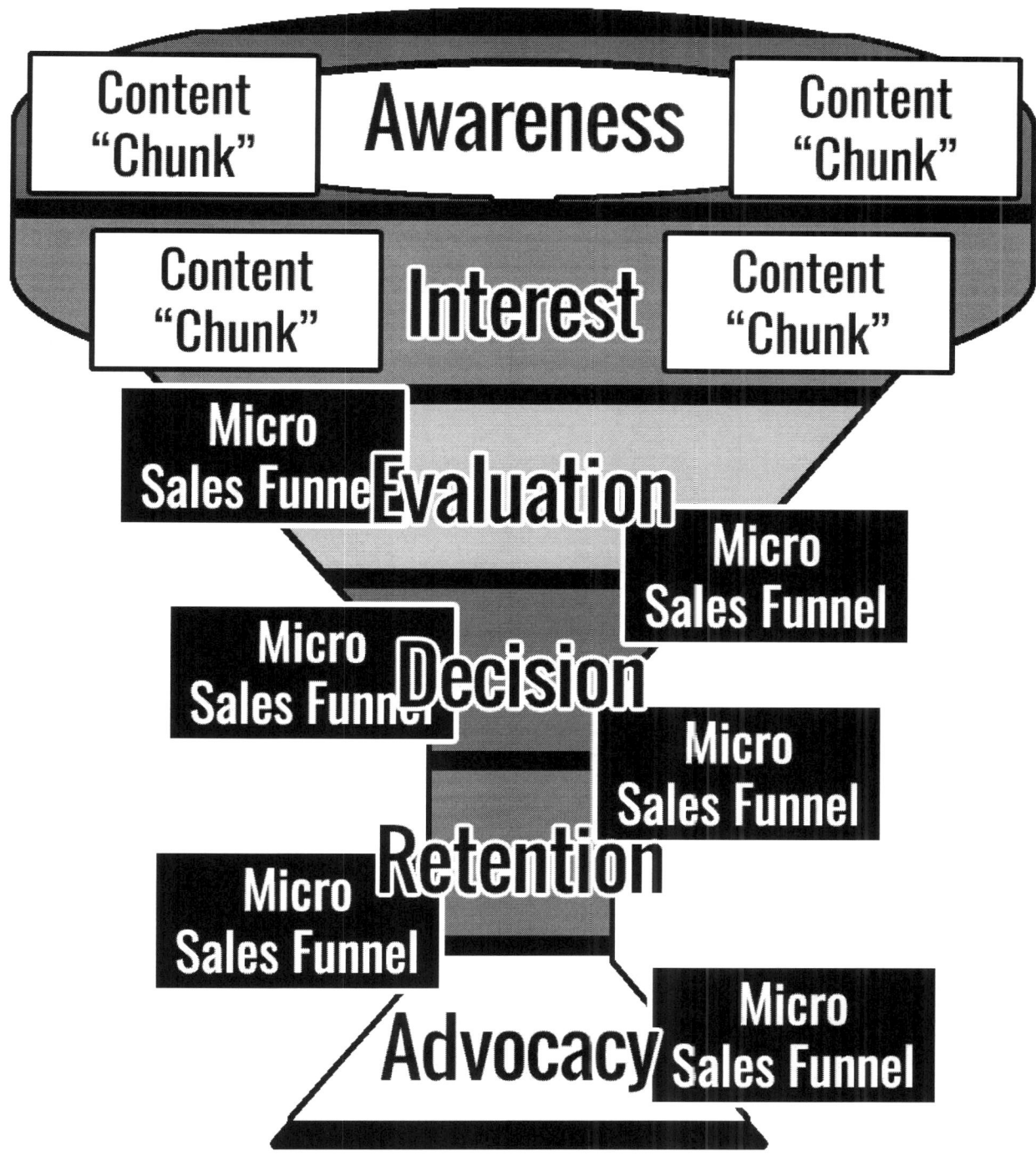

It's starting to look a little crazy, right?!

But, the point is simple. The Main Series and all your Content "Chunks" are figuring out people's interests. Once those interests are known, people flow into various Micro Sales Funnels which take them through the rest of the Macro Sales Funnel.

Without further ado, let's get into these Micro Sales Funnel models!

Sales Page "Funnel"

Let's keep it really simple and start off with your basic Sales Page "Funnel".

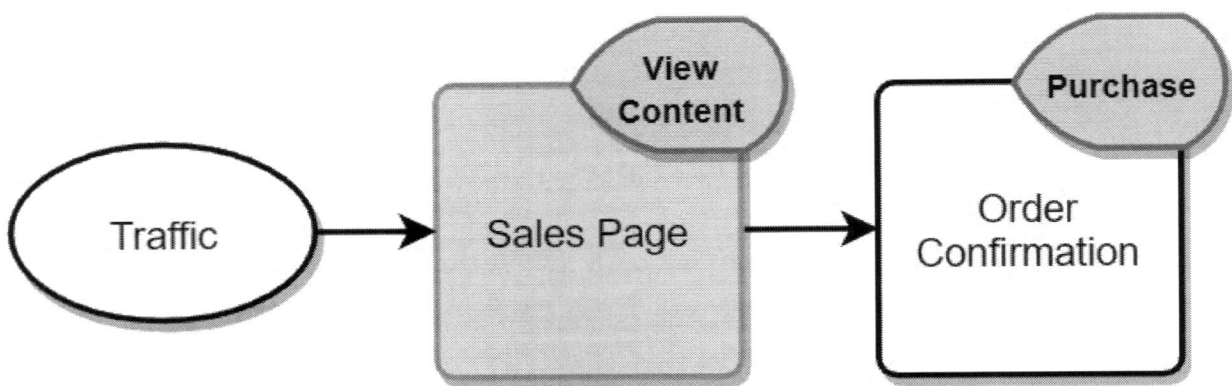

All this "funnel" entails is sending your audience to a Sales Page (a page with an offer on it) and they can either buy that offer and proceed to the Order Confirmation page, or they can leave. It's that simple.

Sales Page Content

You see Sales Pages everywhere online, so this shouldn't take much explaining; however, here's a breakdown of some of the common elements you may want to include on your Sales Page:

- Headline – Only job is to capture attention
- Subheadline – Clarify headline, share main benefit of the offer
- Image – You will likely have a bunch of images on your sales page; however, the very first one should be focused on grabbing attention

- Video – You can use a video instead of an image. In the video, cover the...
    - Who – Who are you?
    - What – What do you have to offer?
    - Why – Why should someone want what you're offering?
    - How – How to get what you're offering.
- Lead Copy – Brief paragraph that pulls the individual into the rest of your sales page
- Trust Signals – Social proof, testimonials, as seen on
- Longer Copy – What you're actually selling. Features, benefits, description of offer (what they get, bonuses, payment options, etc.), etc.
- Call To Action (CTA) – How to get it

Here's an example Sales Page:

Super Awesome Headline For Product

Super Awesome Sub-Headline For Product

"Voted Product Of The Year By Crazy Eye Marketing Magazine!"

 Get Your Super Product!

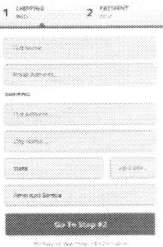

What People Are Saying

 Super Awesome Words About A Super Awesome Product Super Awesome Words About A Super Awesome Product Super Awesome Words About A Super Awesome Product Super Awesome Words About A Super Awesome Product

Super Awesome Words About A Super Awesome Product Super Awesome Words About A Super Awesome Product Super Awesome Words About A Super Awesome Product Super Awesome Words About A Super Awesome Product

Intro sentence to product

Lots of words about product Lots of words about product Lots of words about product Lots of words about product Lots of words about product

Lots of words about product Lots of words about product

✓ **Benefit #1:** Our products are delivered immediately
✓ **Feature #1:** Explain the benefit of your products
✓ **Benefit #2:** Our products are delivered immediately
✓ **Feature #2:** Explain the benefit of your products
✓ **Benefit #3:** Our products are delivered immediately
✓ **Feature #3:** Explain the benefit of your products

Lots of words about product Lots of words about product Lots of words about product Lots of words about product

Lots of words about product Lots of words about product

Yes! I Want Super Product Now!

Fast Action Bonus!

Get This Super Awsome Bonus When You Purchase The Super Awesome Product In The Next...

00 10 33

About The Company/Creator

Lots of words about company/creator Lots of words about company/creator Lots of words about company/creator Lots of words about company/creator

Lots of words about company/creator

✓ **Fact #1:** Our products are delivered immediately
✓ **Fact #2:** Explain the benefit of your products
✓ **Fact #3:** Our products are delivered immediately
✓ **Fact #4:** Explain the benefit of your products

Lots of words about company/creator Lots of words about company/creator Lots of words about company/creator

Lots of words about company/creator

Yes! I Want Super Product Now!

Frequently Asked Questions

Q: What does this watch do?
Really good answer to this question Really good answer to this question Really good answer to this question Really good answer to this question Really good answer to this question Really good answer to this question Really good answer to this question

Q: What does this watch do?
Really good answer to this question Really good answer to this question Really good answer to this question Really good answer to this question Really good answer to this question Really good answer to this question Really good answer to this question

Q: What does this watch do?
Really good answer to this question Really good answer to this question Really good answer to this question Really good answer to this question Really good answer to this question Really good answer to this question Really good answer to this question

Yes! I Want Super Product Now!

100% Money Back Guarantee!

If, for any reason whatsoever, you don't love the watch and find it more valuable than the $19.95 you paid to get it...

We will refund your payment and you can even keep the watch.

There is zero risk.

Order Your Super Product Today!

Why are we offering Super Product at such a discount?
Really good answer to this question Really good answer to this question Really good answer to this question Really good answer to this question Really good answer to this question Really good answer to this question Really good answer to this question

Here's what to do next...
Order your Super Product by clicking the orange button below!

Yes! I Want Super Product Now!

Order Confirmation Page Content

The Order Confirmation page simply confirms their order and may share details about when it will be shipped, how to access the product, how to get support, etc.

But, you can also use your Order Confirmation pages to direct people to more offers by adding an "**offer wall**"!

It's pretty simple, just include a blurb along the lines of "Customers who purchased [the product you just purchased] also purchased products X, Y, and Z." Then, simply link those images/buttons over to the Micro Sales Funnels that sell those particular offers.

Here's an example Order Confirmation Page:

Your Order Is Complete!

Keep An Eye On Your Inbox For Shipping Information!

The Kitty Cat Laser Pointer!

The Purrrfect Cat Brush!

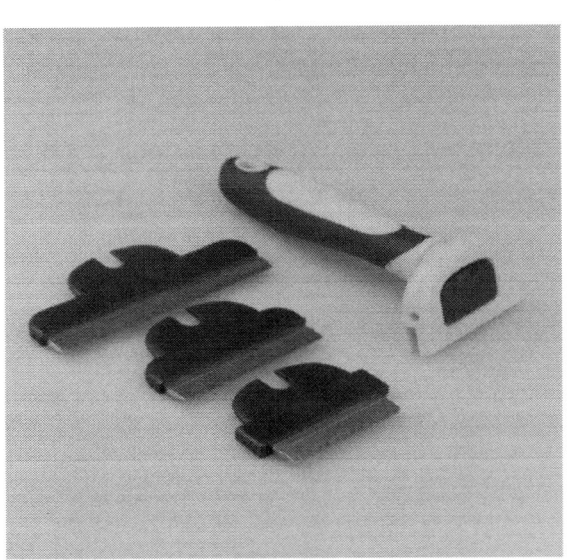

Check Out The Kitty Cat Laser Pointer!

Check Out The Purrrfect Cat Brush!

Trouble? Contact Us!

2-Step / Lead Generation Funnel

The 2-Step / Lead Generation Funnel is used to capture contact information, adding it to one of your various lists and segments, so you can reach out to them again and again.

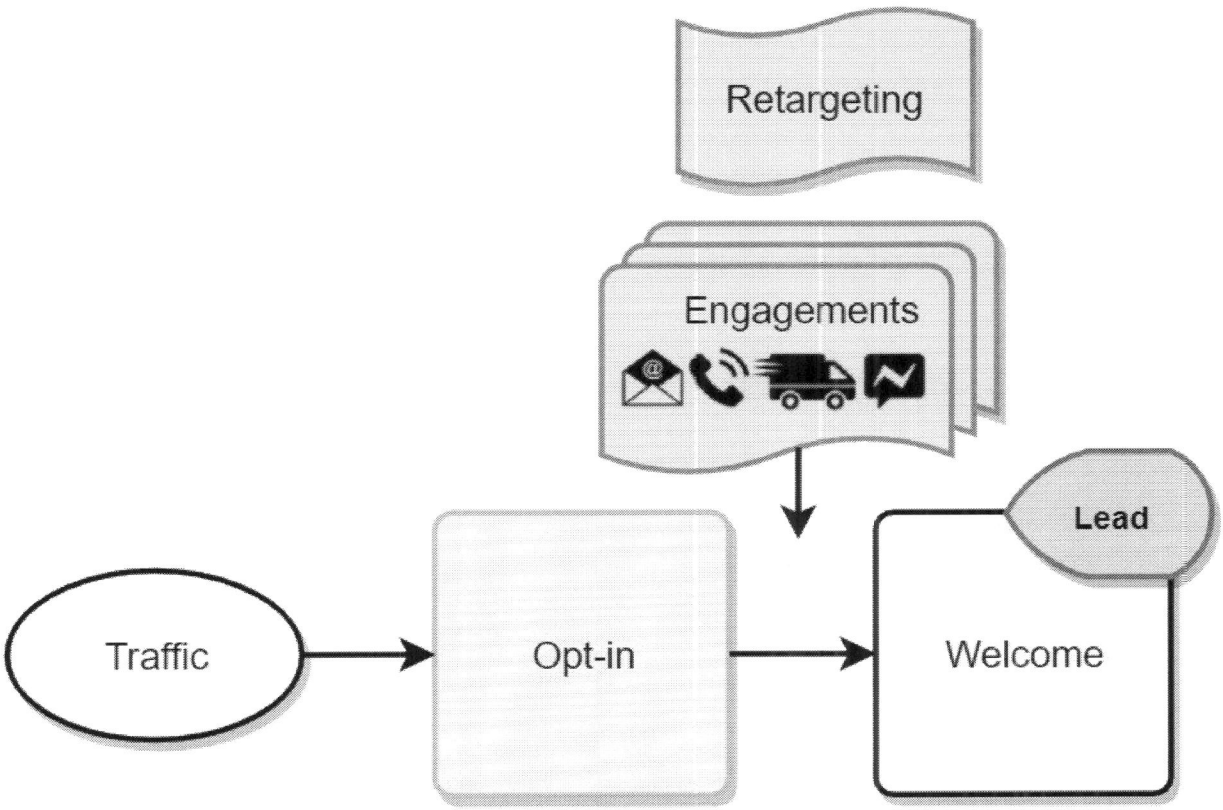

It works like this, send people to an Opt-in Page that requests the individual's contact information in exchange for a Lead Magnet. Once they enter their contact info, they're brought to a Welcome Page and the Lead Magnet is delivered via another medium (email, Facebook Messenger, direct mail, etc.)

Note: The Opt-in Page is also called a Squeeze Page because it "squeezes" the contact information out of someone.

<u>Note 2:</u> A Lead Magnet is simply something of value. It can be an ebook, checklist, trial, flowchart, mp3, video, voucher, etc. Anything someone would give you their contact information to receive.

Opt-in Page Content

When it comes to Opt-In Pages, typically, the simpler the better. A few common elements are listed below:

- Headline – What the lead magnet is
- Subheadline or Bullets – Benefit(s) of the lead magnet
- Image – Show them what the lead magnet looks like or the benefit of it
- Form – A place to enter their contact information
- Submit Button – A way to send their contact information

You typically don't need to get much fancier than that and often it's detrimental to your conversion rates to get much fancier.

That being said, in some instances, making your Opt-in Page look like a Sales Page can produce amazing results.

It's best to have a couple variations of your Opt-in Pages so you can split test them and see which works best for you, your audience, and your offer.

Here's an example Opt-in Page:

Super Awesome Headline For Lead Magnet

Super Awesome Sub-Headline For Lead Magnet

Enter Your Contact Info Below:

| Your Name | 👤 |

| Your Email | ✉️ |

→ Download My Copy Now!

Welcome Page Content

The Welcome Page usually contains a video, but it doesn't have to. At the very least, it should do a couple of things:

- Tell them how to get the Lead Magnet they just requested, ie. Check your email.
- Introduce your business and yourself in order to build some rapport and credibility.

- o A testimonial or two may be helpful (if applicable).
- A walkthrough the Lead Magnet (if applicable).
- Give them the next step (Important!)
  - o Someone just requested a Lead Magnet from you. They're interested in your topic, offer, company, or something else, and you need to keep the momentum going.
  - o Tell them something along the lines of, "While you wait for [Lead Magnet name] to arrive, why don't you checkout this page which contains even more information you'll really enjoy!"

Here's an example Welcome Page:

Check Your Email!

Your Copy Of The Sales Funnel Book Is On Its Way To Your Inbox

What You're About To Learn In This Video...

Super Secret #1

Lorem ipsum dolor sit amet, consectetur adipisicing elit. Non eaque incidunt, quam voluptatem distinctio, dolor aliquam quasi nihil accusamus officiis, ratione necessitatibus vero officia iure iste similique.

Super Secret #2

Lorem ipsum dolor sit amet, consectetur adipisicing elit. Non eaque incidunt, quam voluptatem distinctio, dolor aliquam quasi nihil accusamus officiis, ratione necessitatibus vero officia iure iste similique.

Super Secret #3

Lorem ipsum dolor sit amet, consectetur adipisicing elit. Non eaque incidunt, quam voluptatem distinctio, dolor aliquam quasi nihil accusamus officiis, ratione necessitatibus vero officia iure iste similique.

Super Secret #4

Lorem ipsum dolor sit amet, consectetur adipisicing elit. Non eaque incidunt, quam voluptatem distinctio, dolor aliquam quasi nihil accusamus officiis, ratione necessitatibus vero officia iure iste similique.

→ Go Buy The Complementary Course

Engagement Content

The Engagement Content will vary based on the source, medium, and angle you're delivering it from. At its core, you want to:

- Deliver the promised Lead Magnet
- Welcome them to your business

- Tell them what to do next

Basically, the same stuff you include on your Welcome Page!

Note: See Appendix A for some pre-written email autoresponder series that will help you get started in the right direction.

Merge The 2-Step & Sales Page Funnels

We just discussed Sales Pages and 2-Step / Lead Generation Funnels, the next logical step is to merge the two together.

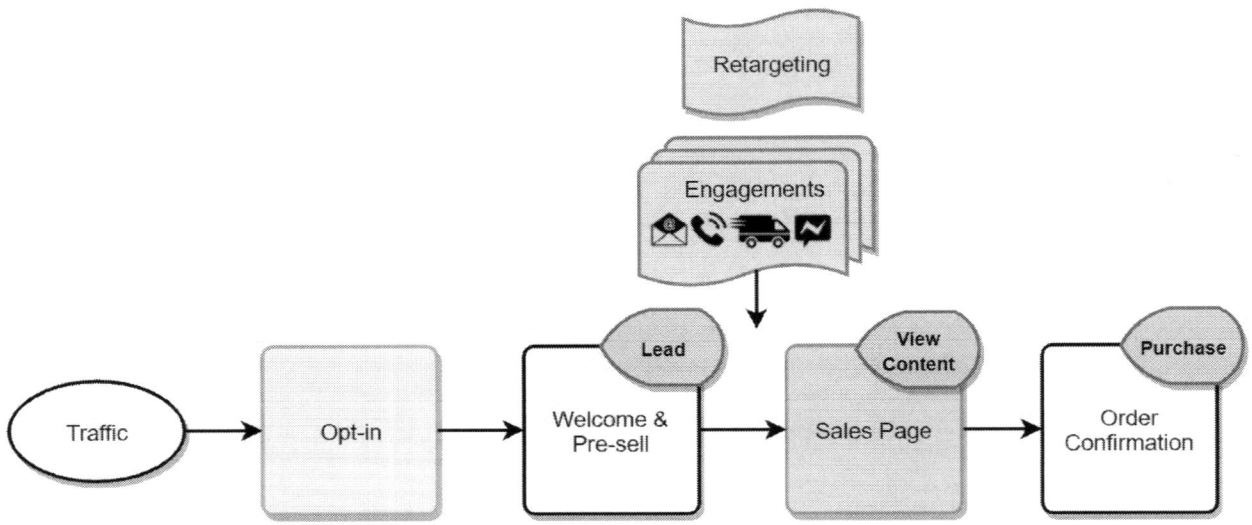

The above diagram should make absolute sense to you now.

You will send traffic to an Opt-in Page, which brings the person to your Welcome & Pre-sell Page, which directs the individual to your Sales Page, which finally takes them to the Order Confirmation Page.

Along the way, the individual is added to various lists and segments (retargeting, email, Facebook Messenger, phone, address, etc.) which gives you the ability to send engagements that "push" them to the Sales Page so they'll hopefully buy your offer.

The Front-End Funnel

The Front-End Funnel goes by many names: Classic Sales Funnel, Trip Wire Funnel, Self Liquidating Funnel, etc. and it's probably the most popular Micro Sales Funnel model.

In fact, McDonalds built their empire based on it with their infamous line, "Would you like fries with that?"

This type of funnel is the true money maker because it directly increases average order value, and thus, lifetime value.

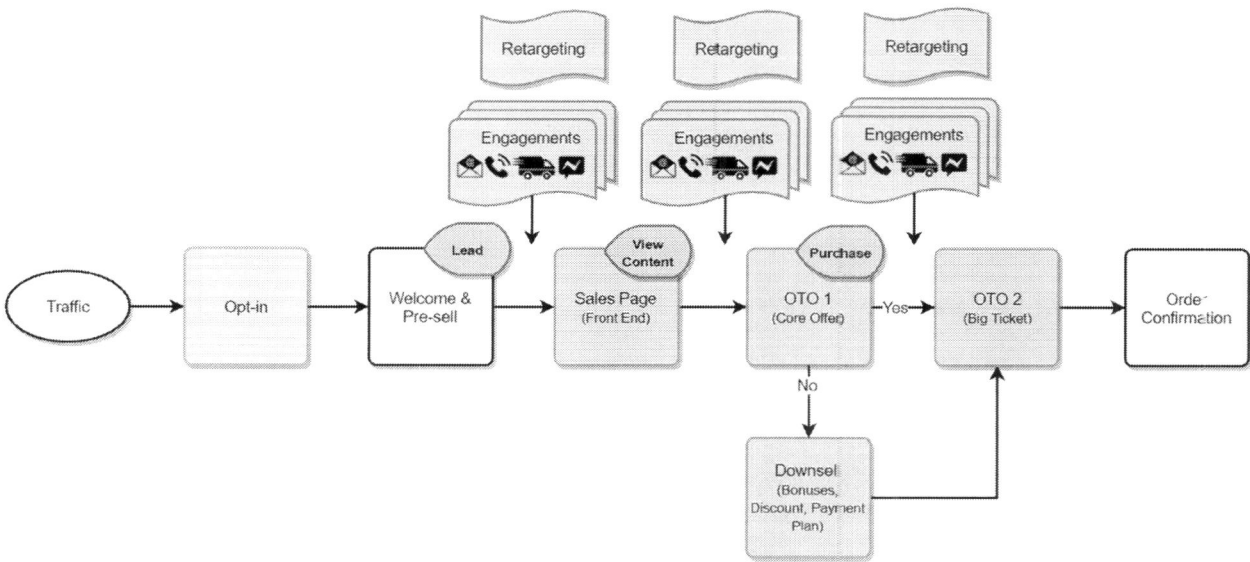

The Opt-in, Welcome & Pre-sell, Sales, and Order Confirmation Pages are similar to what we've already discussed. What's new are the One-Time-Offer (OTO) and Downsell pages.

These are typically 1-click offers, meaning the customer only needs to click one button on these pages to add additional products to their order.

That being said, it doesn't *"have"* to be 1-click offers. You can also connect these upsells and downsells with marketing automation and retargeting. In which case, it could take someone a few days or weeks to progress all the way through your Front-End Funnel.

Also, your Front-End funnel can certainly look different from what's illustrated above, depending on what you have. For example, maybe you only have one OTO, or maybe you don't want to offer a Downsell, or you don't want to have an Opt-in and Welcome Page... that's fine.

Typically, the front-end offer is something at a very low price (<$10) in order to get the individual to open their wallet. Basically, looking for impulse buys. Then, when the "buyer is in heat", they'll buy your OTOs and/or Downsells until you anger them or stop offering things to buy. (that's the theory, anyway)

Conversely, you don't need go after cheap, impulse buys. You could have any offer as your front-end offer, just so long as people buy it.

Think about airlines. If you've ever purchased an airline ticket online, you buy your ticket (front-end offer). Then, they show you some local hotels you might want to stay at (OTO). Then, they show you some rental cars (OTO). And so on.

This type of order flow is very common and you see it everywhere.

OTO Page Content

Again, OTO stands for One-Time-Offer and it's essentially a special offer presented to an individual, only one time, which is *right now!* If they don't act now, they miss out on this exclusive offer forever. This added element of scarcity increases conversions. (Note: your OTOs don't *have* to vanish forever, you can certainly make the offers again, but be ethical about it! Don't say it's going to vanish forever when it really doesn't.)

Your OTO is typically one of these four things:

1. **Your Core Offer**, if you offered a cheap (<$10) impulse offer on the front-end, you may want to offer your "Core Offer" as an OTO. The core offer is the product or service you *actually* want to sell, while the front-end offer is simply to get the person to open their wallet.
2. **A Continuity Offer**, who doesn't want a recurring income? If possible, try to include a continuity offer as an OTO. For example, some type of membership site, community, additional support that's recurring, etc.
3. **A Profit Maximizer**, a really high-priced product or service ($1,000+) that dramatically increases your customer's lifetime value.
4. **A Complementary Offer**, obviously, you can offer any other product or service that complements the front-end offer.

Here's an example OTO Page:

Super Awesome Headline For OTO #1
Super Awesome Sub-Headline For OTO #1

Why You Want This...

Super Secret #1

Lorem ipsum dolor sit amet, consectetur adipisicing elit. Non eaque incidunt. quam voluptatem distinctio, dolor aliquam quasi nihil accusamus officiis, ratione necessitatibus vero officia iure iste similique.

Super Secret #2

Lorem ipsum dolor sit amet, consectetur adipisicing elit. Non eaque incidunt. quam voluptatem distinctio, dolor aliquam quasi nihil accusamus officiis, ratione necessitatibus vero officia iure iste similique.

Super Secret #3

Lorem ipsum dolor sit amet, consectetur adipisicing elit. Non eaque incidunt. quam voluptatem distinctio, dolor aliquam quasi nihil accusamus officiis, ratione necessitatibus vero officia iure iste similique.

Super Secret #4

Lorem ipsum dolor sit amet, consectetur adipisicing elit. Non eaque incidunt. quam voluptatem distinctio, dolor aliquam quasi nihil accusamus officiis, ratione necessitatibus vero officia iure iste similique.

→ YES! Add OTO #1 To My Order!

Your Card Will Be Charged $97.00 Today.

Click Here to say, *"No thanks, I don't want to improve my life."* and turn down this deal

The Video

More often than not, a video will outperform a text-based OTO page, so we're going to use video as the example. However, it's recommended to split-test each and see which works best for your business, audience, and offer.

The video should only be 3-5 minutes in length and hit on a few key points:

- Tell them the Front-End Offer they just grabbed is awesome and they'll have instant access to it in just a minute, or that it's being prepped for shipping, or however you're going to deliver it. Reiterate a key benefit or two.
- Introduce the OTO as a special offer that will make what they just purchased even better.
  - Also, hit on the fact that this offer is not for everyone. It's only for individuals who grabbed the Initial Offer (if applicable).
- Tell them what the OTO is and how it will benefit them.
- Tell them to click the button below to accept the offer.
- If you offer a guarantee, mention it.
- Share a review/testimonial or two. Or at least snippets with the key points.
- Tell them again to click the button below to accept the offer.

If you hit on all of those points, you'll easily fill the 3-5 minutes!

Downsell Page Content

The Downsell Page is the page an individual lands on when they say "no" to the OTO.

Typically, the Downsell Page is used to confirm the fact the individual didn't want your OTO. Think of it as asking, "Are you sure you don't want fries with that?"

Some example downsell offers include:

- **A payment plan**. If your OTO was expensive, you can offer to split the payment up into a few installments. This might make people more apt to buy your OTO since less money is leaving their wallet on day 1. Of course, you could make the payment plan a little more money in your pocket over the long run, for example, instead of $197 up front, it's 3 payments of $77.
- **A lesser version**. If you have a lesser version of your original OTO, you can offer it as a downsell. For example, if you're selling a $200 set of kitchen knives for your OTO, and the customer says "no", the downsell could be a $100 set of knives. They're still knives and still complement the front-end offer, but they're a lesser version from what was initially offered.
- **An incentive**. Offering a bonus or a discount with your OTO downsell could push people over the edge and get them to take you up on your offer.
- **A trial**. Offering a $1 or free trial to your OTO could work here, especially if it's a continuity offer.
- **Ask "are you sure?"** Sometimes, all you need to do is ask people if they're "sure" they want to turn down your OTO. You will want to re-iterate the benefits of the offer and stress how good it is, but sometimes, simply asking them to buy the same offer again, works!

Tip: With the payment plan and lesser version options, it's still a good idea to make the original OTO offer available on the downsell page. Once someone sees the other options, they may be more inclined to take you up on your original offer.

Here's an example downsell page:

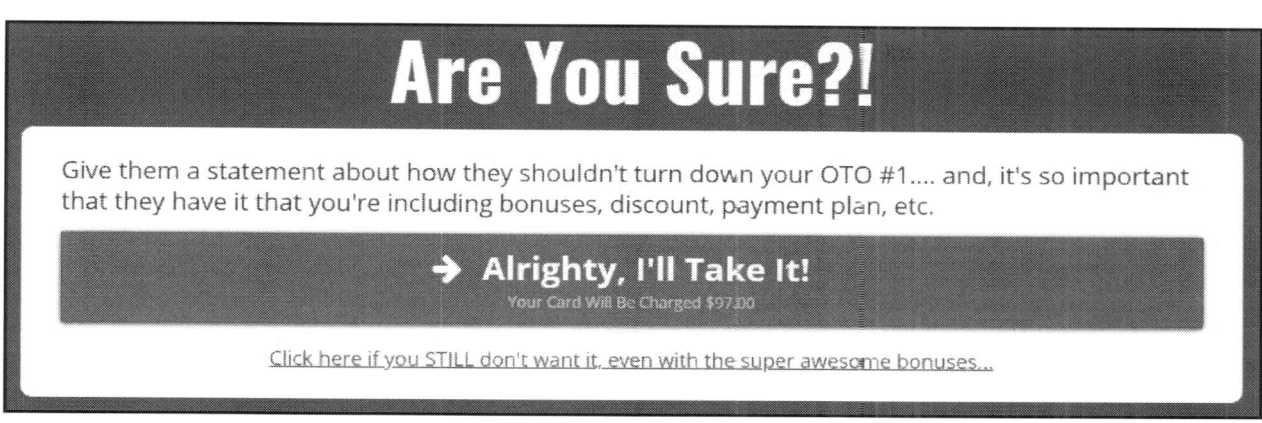

Yes, THAT simple! ↑ ↑ ↑

Engagement Content

The Engagement Content will vary based on the source, medium, and angle you're delivering it from, but at its core, you will want to move individuals through your funnel.

One great way to approach this engagement content is to use **copywriting formulas**.

Everyone loves formulas, right? All you need to do is follow them and boom! You're rich!

Ok, obviously it's not that easy, but formulas get you moving in the right direction.

Fortunately, there are hundreds of copywriting formulas to suit your every need. There are the "tried and true" formulas, some for long form copy like sales pages, others for one sentence ads, and everything in between.

These copywriting formulas work so well because they are deeply rooted in psychology. By following them, you're able to hit on certain psychological cues or angles, that really connect with your leads and customers.

The formulas help you cover all your bases and ensure you don't leave anything out.

Google will be your friend here; simply Google "copywriting formulas" and start looking for one that resonates with you and the product or service you're trying to sell. Some of these formulas have massive write-ups with tons of examples; therefore, you should never feel "stuck".

A Few Popular Copywriting Formulas

Here are a few, very popular, copywriting formulas you may find helpful:

Before-After-Bridge

- **Before** – What life is like *before* your product/service enters it (life sucks)
- **After** – How great life is *after* your product/service is in your audience member's life (life is amazing)
- **Bridge** – Your product/service … aka … How to get to the "after" (here's how to make your life amazing)

Problem-Agitate-Solve

- **Problem** – Identify the problem in your audience member's life (you're wasting so much time)
- **Agitate** – Make the audience member "angrier" about their problem (you're also wasting so much money)
- **Solve** – Present your product/service as the solution to this aggravating problem (save time and money)

Attention-Interest-Desire-Action (AIDA)

- **Attention** – Grab your audience member's attention by being bold (you're going to die sooner than you think)

- **Interest** – Give your audience member interesting information on the problem your product/service solves (mad scientist releases super pill so you won't die)
- **Desire** – Present the benefits of the product/service and provide proof it does what you say (more time with family and friends)
- **Action** – Ask them to buy (buy super pill here)

How To Use The Formulas

As I alluded to earlier, these copywriting formulas can be used in a variety of places. You can use them to help structure your ads, Facebook Messages, letters, text messages, phone calls, and of course - emails.

You will typically use these formulas when creating your Engagement Content for your Front-End Funnels or when you're taking individuals directly to a sales page; however, they can be used most anywhere. Remember, copywriting is all about getting people to take action – which is exactly what we want from these engagements. You're no longer trying to gauge interest, you've done that via the Main Series, Specific Lead Magnet, click, pageview, etc. Now it's time to get the individual to buy something from you.

Note: For the rest of this example, I'm going to relate the formulas to emails; however, the same concepts apply to whichever medium is most relevant to you.

How you'll apply these formulas to your email marketing campaigns will depend on your audience and what you're trying to sell.

Some audiences enjoy receiving long, thorough emails; others want a short blurb with a link to more information.

Complex or expensive products and services tend to take more "convincing" than simple or cheaper products and may require more emails to ensure you cover all the angles.

Here are a few ways to use these powerful copywriting formulas to structure your emails:

1 Short Email

In this scenario, include the entire copywriting formula in one email... in as few sentences as possible.

The goal is to get people to click the link in your email in order to receive more information.

This scenario comes in handy when your audience doesn't read long emails and/or mainly checks their email on a mobile device. They don't have the time to sit and scroll through a long-winded email.

For example (AIDA): Missing out? 99% of small businesses don't have a sales funnel. Stop leaving money on the table! **Click Here to learn more!**

1 Long Email

In this scenario, you would include the entire copywriting formula in one email, but it would be presented in several sentences and paragraphs – more like a sales page.

The goal is to really "sell" in the email. It can even link directly to the order form as opposed to a sales page.

This scenario comes in handy when you want to try a different angle than the normal sales page or if you're trying to sell an affiliate product. (This is a good method when you don't control the sales page, but want to provide as much information as possible in your own voice before sending your subscriber to someone else's sales page.)

Email Series

In this scenario, you break up the copywriting formula across several emails.

The goal is to introduce different angles to the subscriber to drive them to either your sales page or order form.

For example, with the problem-agitate-solve formula, the first email could talk solely about the problem your subscriber is facing. The second email would agitate the problem by relating it to emotion or what they're missing out on by having this problem. The third email lays out the solution, ie. your product or service.

This scenario comes in handy when you're trying to sell something complicated and/or expensive and you need more time to cover the features, benefits, proof, etc.

In Annex A, I've included two pre-written email series that follow proven copywriting formulas. These will help you better understand this concept and get you moving in the right direction!

The Product Launch Funnel

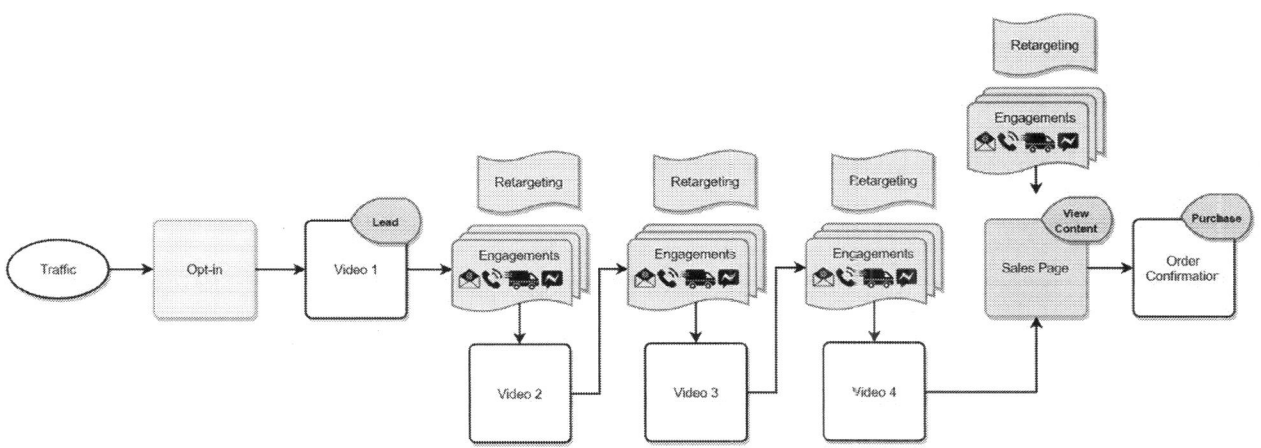

Note: I'm going to mostly reference emails as the engagement medium through this explanation, but as you already know, you can use retargeting, Facebook Messenger, phone calls, texts, even direct mail to move people through your funnel.

The Product Launch Funnel works well for more expensive products, like digital courses.

It's typically three content-based videos, that entertain and educate, and concludes with a fourth video that makes the offer.

The general flow is this:

Someone shows interest in your upcoming product launch by opting-in, clicking a link, viewing a page, etc. – all the normal "interest gauging" triggers.

From there, they receive a few emails or other engagements directing them to video 1. After they watch the first video, they receive emails about video 2. They watch it, and then receive emails about video 3. They watch it and then receive emails to video 4, which is typically a Video Sales Letter (VSL).

The power behind this funnel comes from two key aspects:

First, this funnel provides insane value in videos 1-3 by giving away your "best stuff". If you do these videos correctly, it will make your offer a no-brainer. People will think, "If his free stuff is this amazing... I can't imagine how *absolutely incredible* his paid stuff is!"

The second source of this funnel's power comes from the Launch / Cart Open phase. During this phase, scarcity is introduced because **the cart will close**.

There are a few ways to close the cart. The way you do it depends on whether your Product Launch Funnel is a true, one-time event or if it's evergreen (always available).

If it's a true, one-time event, then it's easy to introduce scarcity because you're going to take the offer off the table at a certain date and time. If the individual misses it, too bad.

If it's an evergreen launch, you need to introduce scarcity in another manner because you won't be removing the offer. You can do this by removing bonuses or by increasing the price if they don't purchase by a certain date.

The Video Pattern

Before I go any further, I want to address something – I keep saying "video"; however, you don't necessarily need videos. You could use other resources like blog posts or PDFs to develop a product launch funnel.

Videos are often used because digital video courses are typically sold during a product launch funnel. It makes sense to keep everything in the same medium.

With that being said, you should follow a pattern or strategy for delivering the first three videos. There's some psychology and positioning at play.

There's a proven science behind this approach and there are folks that make millions regularly from these product launch funnels.

While I'll give you my particular formula in a moment, I want to share two other guys' formulas… or at least where to get them. (It wouldn't be ethical, and it's probably illegal, to just paste their formulas here; however, you can get them straight from the books I'm about to recommend. Each book is less than $10, but contains invaluable information.)

- Jeff Walker's *"Launch"*: http://www.thelaunchbook.com/

- o Pages 89-97
- Russel Brunson's *"DotCom Secrets"*: https://dotcomsecretsbook.com/
  - o Pages 222-227

My Formula: Teach, To-Do, & Tease

While I typically follow the aforementioned formulas because they know what they're doing, I sometimes find them hard to follow. They require certain information to be presented, like success stories.

Success stories are important, and you need to have people find success with your product; however, there's a chicken and egg situation here. You can't really have success stories (besides your own) before your product exists, right?

While you can do a limited pre-launch to get feedback and success stories, doing so takes time and requires an audience.

If you're short on time and/or lack an audience, what I'm about to explain may work very well for you!

I call it the "Teach, To-Do, & Tease" formula. In each video, you teach something, give the individual a simple task, and tease what's to come.

I'll explain this formula through an example.

Let's pretend I'm selling an expensive course titled, "How to Become a World-Class Facebook Ads Guru".

Across the Product Launch Funnel, I would teach a segment of the course.

Which segment? Either the "coolest" part or the beginning. Sometimes you can't teach the "coolest" part because your course is progressive and you can't do the "cool" stuff without having completed steps 1-5 first.

You also want to ensure the segment you teach **provides a clear deliverable**.

Think of it like a mini-course with a beginning, middle, and end.

Basically, whether or not they purchase the full course, I want them to receive at least one clear result from my training.

You never want to leave anyone feeling like they've been duped... like they have been drug along just to be sold your product.

You want them to accomplish *something*, and if they want more – there's a full course on the topic.

Back to the example, regarding Facebook Ads, I can't start with the "cool" stuff because without having the proper groundwork in place, the "cool" stuff can't happen.

The segment taught is the beginning and it's titled, "How to build custom audiences that know, like, and trust you with Facebook's advertising platform."

In video 1, I'll teach people how to install the Facebook tracking pixel on their website, tell them to go do it, and tease the conversion tracking training coming in video 2.

In video 2, I'll teach them how to track conversions and create custom conversions which will help them create custom audiences... which is covered in video 3.

In video 3, I'll teach them how to create custom audiences based on pages viewed, conversions made, and how to use this to create lookalike audiences of similar people that will know, like, and trust you!

Finally, in video 4, I'll pitch the full course by explaining how what they just learned will help them tremendously moving forward; however, it's only a small segment of becoming a World-Class Facebook Ads Guru!

See how it's all a natural flow into selling the full product? It doesn't require having testimonials and success stories because you're helping them find success!

If you help someone solve a problem for free, they're more likely to reciprocate later on down the road when they have another problem you can help solve. They will want to give you money.

Video Page Content

We've already discussed all the pages in this funnel with the exception of the Video Pages.

These pages should be very simple. All they have to do is deliver the video!

You can also tease the upcoming videos and have a place for people to ask questions.

Here's an example Video Page:

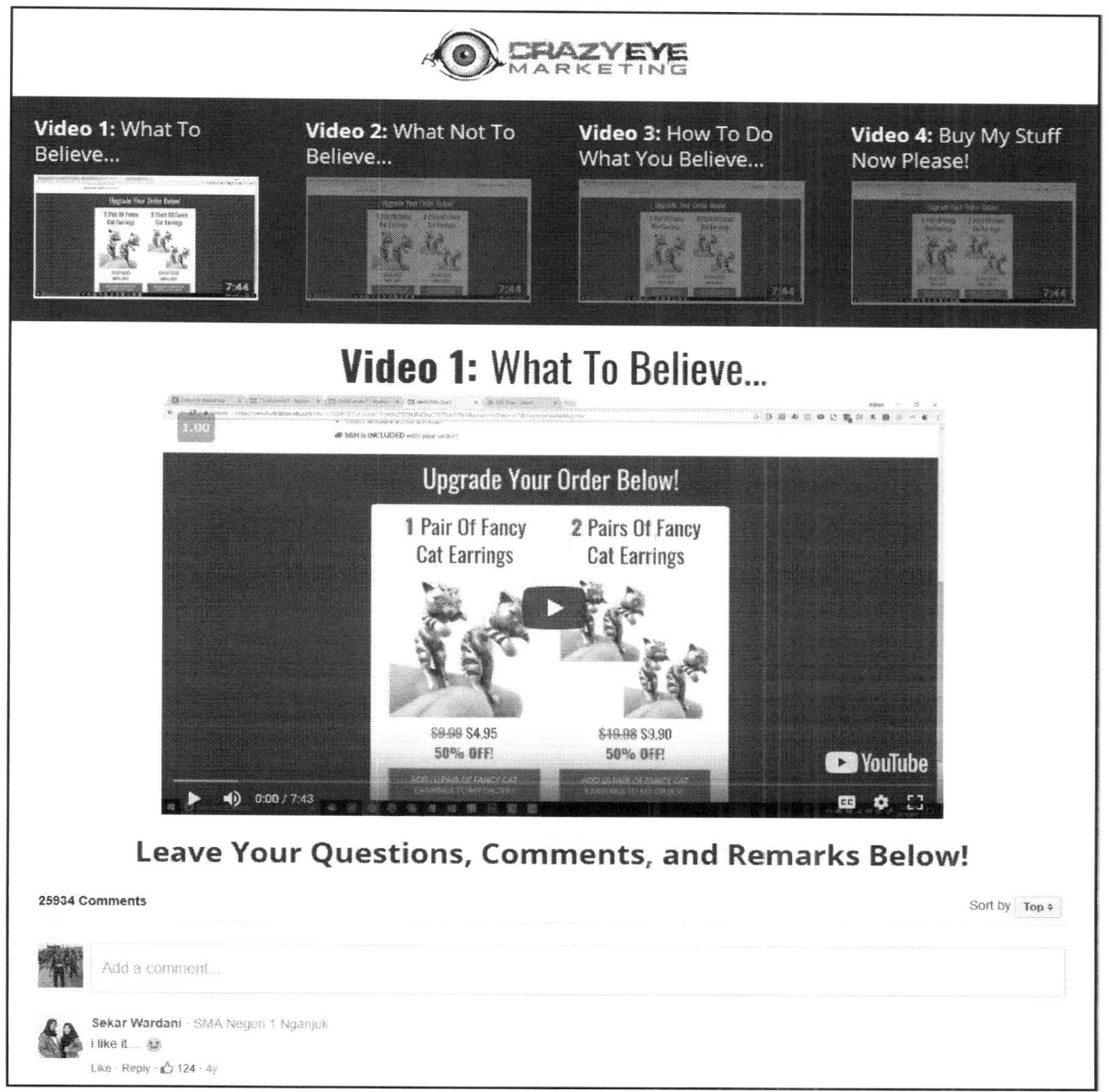

Engagement Content

The content for your engagements that promote your videos should be very simple. The individual is already expecting some videos from you, so it should be pretty natural and seamless to be like, "The next video is up! In it we cover X, Y, and Z! Click here to watch it!"

Now, hopefully, the first three videos get people so excited that when you send video four, they're ready to buy whatever it is you're selling;

unfortunately, this isn't always the case. You may need to be a little more strategic when it comes to the sales or cart opening/closing portion.

First things first, you will want to let people know video four is available, just like you did with the other videos. But, you will also want to include the fact that your offer is now open and will be closing in X hours.

Then, you will want to send more engagements, across every possible medium you can – retargeting, email, Facebook Messenger, text messaging, phone calls, direct mail... don't let anyone miss the fact your offer is available!

To help with these extra engagements, I recommend using the copywriting formulas that were mentioned in the Front-End Funnel section on page 46. Also, use common sense here. Promote testimonials and success stories, crush the objections, re-iterate the value your offer is going to bring into the individual's life or business, mention your ironclad guarantee, etc.

Finally, if Product Launch Funnels sounds like your cup of tea, you should get Jeff Walker's Launch book from http://www.thelaunchbook.com/. He is the master of these funnels and you will learn a lot in his book!

The Webinar Funnel

In the good ol' days, people and businesses hosted more seminars, but now they can get in front of more people faster and easily via webinars.

These types of sales funnels have become wildly popular recently due to the fact they convert like gangbusters!

Here's a common Webinar Sales Funnel:

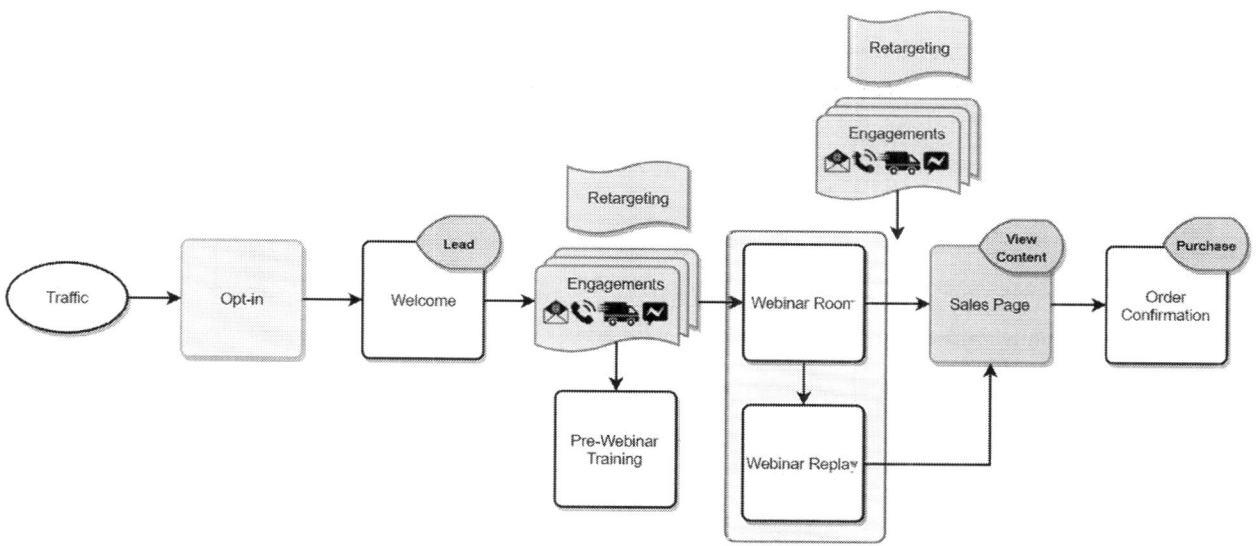

Similar to the Product Launch Funnel, the Webinar Funnel is typically used for higher-priced products and services because people are spending 60+ minutes with you. This gives you enough time to convey your message fully, give the pitch, and answer questions.

While you can automate your webinar to make it evergreen, the live aspect gives these presentations their power.

When it's live, everything comes across as fresh and when you give your call-to-action, there's an inherent sense of urgency. You're ending the presentation at X time, and once it's over, the deal is gone.

The general flow is this:

Someone shows interest in your webinar by opting-in via a webinar registration page. They're then enrolled in your "pre-webinar" series where you send a few videos and resources to prime and excite the individual for the upcoming webinar. Then, you host your webinar.

Ideally, the individual attends your webinar, sees your offer, purchases it, and ends the Micro Sales Funnel.

But, if they don't attend your webinar, you can send a "replay series" which consists of a few engagements (retargeting, email, Facebook

Messenger, text, etc.) that present the individual the opportunity to watch a replay of the webinar.

Hopefully they watch the replay, see your offer, purchase it, and end the Micro Sales Funnel.

If they don't watch the webinar or the replay, they won't see the offer, so this particular Micro Sales Funnel is ended.

If the individual sees the offer, either during the live webinar or the replay, but doesn't purchase it, you can follow up with some engagements following a copywriting formula like the ones mentioned in the Front-End Funnel section on page 46.

Or, you can obviously write your own engagements that answer more questions, handle objections, share more success stories, or even offer a discount in a last-ditch effort to make the sale.

Turning It Evergreen

While the great power of webinars comes from being live, you can still create the same live feel while simultaneously automating the entire process.

By turning your webinar into an evergreen presentation, you're able to give presentations 24/7/365!

There are a million different tools to help you do this; however, there are two elements a tool can't provide that you must take into account before going the evergreen route.

First, the webinar you turn evergreen **needs to be a recorded live webinar**.

This means you can't sit in your office, record yourself talking about some slides, editing the clip to cut out the "uhs", and then launch your evergreen webinar.

Remember, the power of webinars comes from being *live*. People can tell in a heartbeat if something was scripted and performed alone vs. held live.

If someone attends your webinar and they're presented with a scripted presentation, it will come across as unauthentic.

Don't get me wrong, scripted, pre-recorded, and edited presentations are fine; however, call it a presentation, training, or master class – don't call it a webinar.

A webinar has the connotation of being live and if you don't fulfill that, people aren't going to be as happy and excited.

Plus, there are benefits of performing live. You see what does and doesn't work, what questions people have, etc. – it really helps to refine your presentation.

The strategy, then, is to hold a handful of live webinars, get some real time feedback, adjust your presentation, then record one and use it as your evergreen webinar.

The second element you need to provide is **a way to contact you**, the presenter. This can be something as simple as a chat box below the webinar.

As much as humanly possible, no matter if the webinar itself is pre-recorded, you want to be live in the chat room to field any questions.

Some people are ready to buy; however, they will have the simplest question stopping them from whipping out their credit card. If you're able to answer their question immediately – you'll get yourself a new customer!

Live chat may not always be possible, especially if you're running webinars 24/7/365, so the second best option is to follow up via email;

however, you lose the "in the moment" momentum, which may result in lost sales.

Either way, you need to make yourself available as much as possible, even if the webinar itself is recorded.

The Webinar Presentation

Just like with the Product Launch Funnel, there's an art and science behind the content you present in your webinar.

Before you launch your own webinar, make sure you attend a bunch of webinars – especially those in the same niche as you **that you know are successful**.

Since launching a webinar is a piece of cake, every small business on the planet has one. Unfortunately, not all are successful and you don't want to emulate those.

Attend the successful ones. Take notes on how they open, present their content, and pitch their offer.

Understand how they engage with their audience and handle objections.

Pay attention and really study what they do. It's going to help you tremendously.

Finally, I recommend grabbing Russell Brunson's Perfect Webinar training from https://perfectwebinarsecrets.com/.

It costs less than $5 and contains about three hours of training. He outlines, step-by-step, how to structure your webinar presentation for maximum effectiveness.

Conclusion

The Webinar Sales Funnel is an effective way to sell higher end products and services. They give you enough time to go into detail on your offer plus the live aspect makes them very engaging.

Having the ability to answer questions and squash objections on the spot makes them incredibly powerful.

There's also the opportunity to make them evergreen so they're working for your 24/7/365. But, when you turn a webinar evergreen, make sure it's a recorded live version and make yourself available to answer questions.

Finally, before launching your own webinar, make sure you study other successful webinars to really get a good grasp on how to present yours.

The Consultation/Application Funnel

While Product Launch and Webinar Funnels are great for selling many types of high-ticket products and services, sometimes you really need to talk to the individual before they feel comfortable making the purchase.

Other times, you need to feel comfortable selling them the product or service. You may want to qualify them before moving forward on a deal.

Naturally, these situations typically entail talking to the potential customer/client, which is why we have the Consultation/Application Sales Funnel:

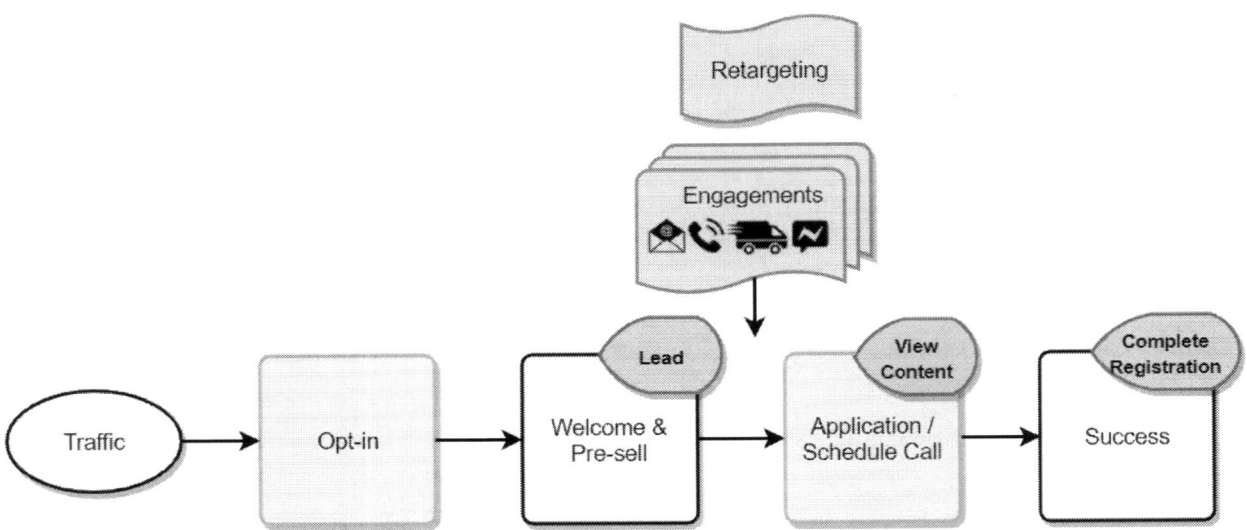

This funnel doesn't have to be complex. The "Contact Us" page on your website can theoretically be your Consultation/Application funnel, but if you want to be more strategic about it, you certainly can.

The concepts behind your Opt-in and Welcome & Pre-sell pages are the same as they've always been; however, the strategy behind them will change a little bit. More on this in just a minute.

Then, you have your Application/Schedule page. This page should contain a form or link to your calendar so they can request a time to speak with you. You may also want to incorporate a few engagements that "push" individuals to this page.

Finally, there's the Success Page which confirms they're scheduled and may contain information on how to prepare for the call.

The Lead Magnet

If you're using a Lead Magnet to generate high quality leads, the strategy behind your Lead Magnet will change compared to when you're just attracting "general" leads. Passing out a simple one-page checklist without much context isn't going to cut it here.

This Lead Magnet needs to be a bit more complete – it needs a beginning, middle, and end. Ultimately, it should be around 10 pages long. This way, it's long enough to "prove" you know what you're doing and it's short enough that the individual may actually consume the whole thing.

To help put you on the right track, here's a framework you can follow:

- Introduction and explanation of the problem
  - Relate to your prospect
  - Present yourself as an authority. How did you figure this whole thing out?
- Give the solution
  - Sections and sub-sections
- "Pitch" the call or application

And, here's an example of that framework for a Lead Magnet called "How To Start A New Business In 8 Weeks Without Wasting Countless Hours And Blowing $1,000s Of Dollars":

- Introduction and explanation of the problem
  - [problem] There are so many guru strategies and tactics for starting a business online that it's hard to know what actually works
  - [intro/background/authority] I personally spent two years floundering online. At one point I lost everything and had to get a regular 9-5 job. But, I kept at it, figured out the Interest Driven Sales Funnel Strategy which helped me grow my business, quit that day job, and now I'm living the dream!
- Give the solution
  - Master ClickFunnels (weeks 1-3)
    - Types of funnels for different products/services
    - Results/proof it works
  - Master ActiveCampaign (weeks 4-6)

- Types of automations and how they work to sell products
- Give away a few pre-written email automation series
    - Master Facebook Ads (weeks 6-8)
        - Types of campaigns
        - Triple threat strategy to decrease customer acquisition costs (results)
- "Pitch" the call or application
    - Want to spend an hour with me to develop a customized Interest Driven Sales Funnel Blueprint for your business? It's FREE!

Welcome & Pre-Sell Page

Your Welcome & Pre-Sell page may also be a little different than in the other funnels because you may want to include client testimonials and results.

Here's an example Welcome & Pre-Sell Page:

Are YOU Ready To Join Us?

I Will PERSONALLY Work With You One-On-One To Help You X, Y, and Z!

→ Click Here To Apply NOW!

Very Limited Openings...

What Our Clients Have To Say...

→ Click Here To Apply NOW!

Since most people won't consume the Lead Magnet you send them (which kind of sucks, because you will have put a lot of time and effort into this one and it positions you and your business as an authority), the first video on the page typically covers the material enclosed in your Lead Magnet, but in greater detail. This video can be anywhere from 5-60+ minutes.

Again, the point of this video is to position yourself as an authority. When you're an authority, you can charge higher prices and be more selective on who you take on, so you have better clients. It's definitely worth taking the time to properly position yourself.

The other videos on the page should be video testimonials. I recommend having a set of questions to ask people, so your testimonials hit on the key elements to help you increase conversions.

You can find video testimonial questions by conducting a Google Search for "video testimonial questions". Also, here's a few questions from Copyblogger:

- What was the obstacle that would have prevented you from buying this product?
- What did you find as a result of buying this product?
- What specific feature did you like most about this product?
- What are three other benefits of this product?
- Would you recommend this product? If so, why?
- Is there anything you'd like to add?

Source: https://www.copyblogger.com/testimonials-part-2/

Finally, you will want to include Calls To Action (CTA) on the page that bring individuals over to your application or calendar.

Application/Schedule Page

The Application/Schedule Page is exactly what you think it is:

There are many ways to make these forms; however, at the time of this writing, Google Forms (https://www.google.com/forms/about/) and Wufoo (https://www.wufoo.com/) are two of the most widely used.

In terms of calendar/scheduling tools, Calendly (https://calendly.com/) is currently the most popular.

Engagements

I mentioned these in a previous section, but your engagements should bring individuals to your Application/Schedule Page because they've already opted-in for your Lead Magnet, they've already seen your Welcome & Pre-Sell Page, but for some reason they haven't filled out your form.

I recommend placing your video testimonials in front of these people through all mediums available (retargeting, email, Facebook Messenger, etc.) you want to remind them that you and your business are awesome and they should schedule a call with you ASAP!

Other Funnels

As I stated at the beginning of this section, every sales funnel "guru" has their own sales funnel model(s) they teach.

This is great! More people to learn from and more models to follow and implement.

Even greater, they all work with the Interest Driven Sales Funnel concept – they're all [typically] Micro Sales Funnels.

You still incorporate your interest gauging Main Series and when interest in a product or service is shown, instead of launching one of the Micro Sales Funnels outlined above, you simply launch that particular "guru's" funnel.

After the individual has gone through that funnel, they hop back into the Main Series and continue their journey until they show interest in something else.

The Interest Driven Sales Funnel concept is very plug & play friendly. I want you to try other Micro Sales Funnels. If you come across one that sounds interesting, try it. If it doesn't work, you can always cut that Micro Sales Funnel off and add in a new one for the same product or service.

Here are a few funnel "gurus" that you may find insightful (no particular order):

- **Russell Brunson** – Founder of ClickFunnels. Has written several books on sales funnels. Has dozens of Micro Sales Funnel models, plus talks about stacking (combining) them for maximum effectiveness. He has too many products and resources to list and all of them are great, just Google him.

- **Aaron Fletcher** – Has the "Fletcher Method" and the "One Page Marketing Funnel". The Fletcher Method is an ideology behind structuring your business and creating great offers. If you're struggling with figuring out what to offer, I recommend checking out his method. His One Page Marketing Funnel is essentially a Product Launch Funnel; however, he incorporates retargeting, phone calls, and even snail mail which make it more effective. Learn more at http://fletchermethod.com/
- **Ezra Firestone** – One of the top ecommerce marketers on the planet. He shares a ton and is always optimizing his funnels with the latest and greatest technologies. You can learn more about his strategies at https://smartmarketer.com
- **Trey Lewellen** – Has made more money than anyone else using Russell Brunson's tool, ClickFunnels. He primarily sells tchotchke items through Front-End Funnels and even teaches people how to do it. If that interests you, be sure to check him out at https://treylewellen.com
- **Ryan Deiss** – Owns more companies than I can count and all are powered by very solid sales funnels. Like Russell Brunson, he has a lot of stuff to offer and is worth a Google search. He teaches all his digital marketing strategy through https://www.digitalmarketer.com/
- **Todd Brown** – Another sales funnel "guru" worth checking out. He has a bunch of different Micro Sales Funnel models that he teaches, all with his unique spin. Learn more about Todd and his funnels at http://marketingfunnelautomation.com/
- **Traffic and Funnels** – A heavy focus on developing client acquisition systems, similar to the "Call / Application Funnel" I

outlined above. If you offer higher end products or services that require conversation, you may find their training to be incredibly helpful. Learn more at http://trafficandfunnels.com/

Those are just some of the people I follow with regard to sales funnels. Of course, there are many others out there and if you find someone that really resonates with you, follow them!

Combining Funnels

As if the possibilities for Micro Sales Funnels weren't already endless, in this section, we'll briefly discuss combining them to make them even more effective!

In general, the Front-end Funnel is the perfect addition to most Product Launch and Webinar Funnels because it makes perfect sense to combine the two:

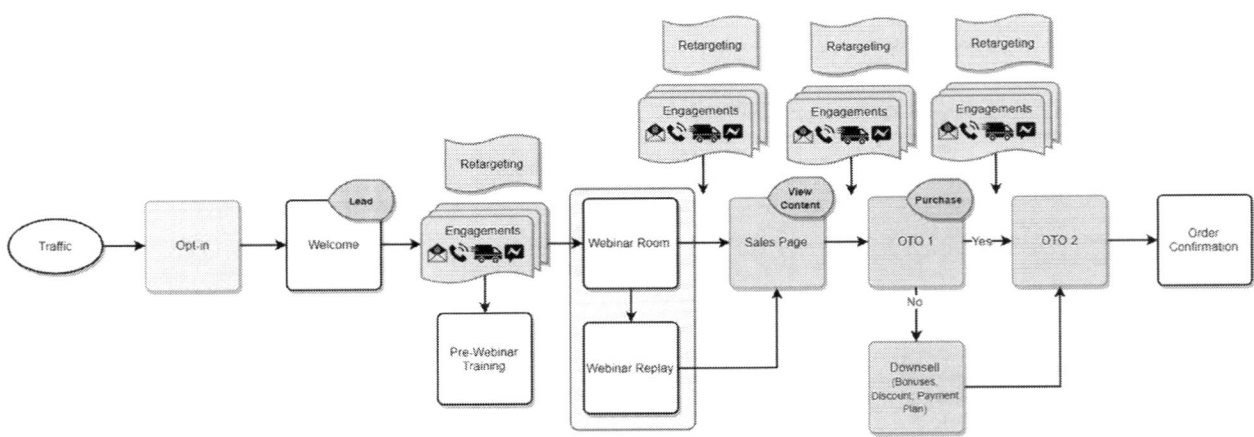

That funnel diagram should make sense, right? You have your webinar and hopefully they buy your initial offer.

Then, immediately afterwards, you can offer complementary products or services like advanced coaching or consulting, or a mastermind.

Think Beyond Webpages

This is a small section that could be easily passed over; however, it's **CRITICALLY IMPORTANT** which is why I just capitalized, bolded, and underlined those words: I want you to understand that Micro Sales Funnels aren't just online, they're everywhere.

MICRO SALES FUNNELS ARE EVERYWHERE!

All of the Micro Sales Funnels outlined in this chapter focus on webpages; however, you certainly don't need them to make your funnels. The same strategies and concepts will always apply and you can build funnels in most any medium – direct mail, Facebook messenger, in person, over the phone, etc.

I'm going to bring up McDonalds again and the "would you like fries with that" line. There are no pages. There's no Internet. It's simply someone taking an order and asking questions to increase Average Order Value (AOV) and, thus, Customer Lifetime Value (CLV).

Another example is seminars, ie. the "original" webinar. On the local radio, I hear ads all the time for local events and seminars. When you go to one of these events, they pitch you on something and are prepared to take your money at the event. Then, depending on what it is you purchased, they may deliver it via mail a few weeks later and in that package is an OTO for an even bigger, more impressive offer. Again, no webpages and no Internet in this example, but it's still a Micro Sales Funnel.

Finally, I don't know what the future holds, but as of this writing, Facebook Messenger just began allowing payments and I've seen businesses create full Micro Sales Funnels using just Facebook Messenger.

So, again, think beyond webpages when building your Micro Sales Funnels.

Now What?

Books are great.

They teach you so much nifty stuff and usually leave you feeling like you've accomplished a great task...

Then reality sets in and you realize you've produced nothing.

Would you trust a brain surgeon who has only read a book on brain surgery? Someone who hasn't at least practiced on pig brains or something?

I know I wouldn't.

Not that sales funnels are as complex as brain surgery, but they still require practice.

They still require work.

You're not going to multiply your revenue by simply consuming.

You have to take action.

Start small.

Start building your various lists.

Start promoting interest gauging content via a Main Series.

Start structuring your products and services in ways you can easily up-sell, down-sell, and cross-sell.

Finally, if you're ready to streamline the funnel building process, I have a program called The Sales Funnel Training Vault available at https://www.crazyeyemarketing.com/join.

All the best to you and your business!

Annexes

ANNEX A: Pre-Written Email Series

Welcome Series

Email #1

Timeframe:

- Immediately or a couple hours after subscribed (if using concurrent email series)

Subject lines:

- Per your request: [lead magnet]
- Here's your download
- As you requested ... [lead magnet]
- Welcome!
- As expected
- Nice to meet you!

Content:

[name]!

If you did not collect the name, use "Hi!" or any other saying that means "hello".

I prefer to deliver upon my promises before anything else ... so as promised, **Click here to download your copy of [lead magnet name]!**

Here's the deal. We know you receive a *ton* of email every day and really struggle to get through it all.

And, you know what? That's OK.

We tend to share "almost" everything on social media as well. So, if you don't want to miss out on any exclusive sales, offers, contests, products, gifts [edit to fit your business], you can get updates by following us on your favorite social media platforms:

Like us on Facebook [link to Facebook]

Follow us on Twitter [link to Twitter]

Follow us on Pinterest [link to Pinterest]

+1 us on Google+ [link to Google+]

[include whatever social media networks you're active on]

Finally, here's what you can expect from us:

* This part is a bit open … include what your subscribers can expect *

ie. X emails, X times per week containing articles that will help you solve ["whatever" problem your business/products/services solve]

Sound good?!

Excellent.

Approximately **24 hours** from now you'll receive another email from me with 3 random facts! **Don't miss it.**

Again, welcome and enjoy!

[your name]

[http://yoursite.com]

Email #1.5

Note:

- Only use this email if you want replies and <u>only</u> if you will respond to those replies.
- This email is meant to come from the CEO/Founder of the company and it's to come across as a personal email from that individual.
- Also, send this email as a text based email. There should be no pictures, no pretty fonts or colors, no borders or margins. Straight text like if you opened up your email client and wrote an email to a friend.

Timeframe:

- 97 minutes after Email #1

Subject lines:

- Quick question

Content:

What's the one biggest problem holding you back from [accomplishing whatever goal your business helps people accomplish]?

One to two sentences would be great!

[your name]

[your title]

Email #2

Timeframe:

- 24 hours after Email #1

Subject lines:

- 3 facts

- Did you know?
- [Your Business Name] EXPLAINED!

Content:

Hi [name],

There are a lot of mysteries.

There's Bigfoot, the Loch Ness Monster, UFOs, and the Lost City of Atlantis.

But, this email is all about cold hard facts.

Real quick! Let me introduce myself / my team with a picture!

[insert picture of yourself / your employees]

Use the line that makes sense for your picture:

- Yup, that's me ... the person behind most of these emails. My name is [your name] and I'm the [your position] here at [your business name] and I'm honored you've allowed me into your inbox!
- Yup, that's my team! They're the awesome individuals responsible for making the business run smoothly in order to better support you. If you ever need assistance, you now know who you're working with!

Now that you know who's behind this email, it's time to share the **3 facts** about [your business name].

Share 3 facts about your business that people wouldn't know at first glance. Here are a few ideas you can hit on:

- Charities you support
- Events you host
- Biggest success story from your clients

- Where the idea for your business came from
- How'd your business get started
- That you have 3 dogs named, Max, Mark, and Mike

1. Fact 1

2. Fact 2

3. Fact 3

Of course, you probably want to learn a little more about us, which is why we have an **"About Us" page that you can visit!** [link to your "About Us" page]

I know I said this email was about cold hard facts. But, a little mystery here and there is a good thing! It keeps us on our toes.

I will be sending you an email tomorrow; however, the topic is a mystery!

Until tomorrow,

[your name]

[http://yoursite.com]

Email #3

Timeframe:

- 24 hours after Email #2

Subject lines:

- The mystery email
- Solved!
- This will help

Content:

Hello [name],

Yesterday I told you I'd be sending an email whose contents were a mystery.

You've patiently waited for this email, and I promise … it's going to help you **bigtime!**

Here are the top 3 articles on our site that will help you [solve whatever problem your business solves for people]:

1. Title and link to article

2. Title and link to article

3. Title and link to article

If that's not enough, know that **we're always here to help you**.

We're one quick email (youremail@yourbusiness.com) or phone call (123-456-7890) away!

We'll be in touch,

[your name]

[http://yoursite.com]

Problem-Agitate-Solve

Email #1

Timeframe:

- Immediately or a couple hours after subscribed (if using concurrent email series)

Subject lines:

- Per your request: [lead magnet]
- Here's your download
- As you requested... [lead magnet]
- [Symptom of problem]?
- [Problem your product/service solves]
- 99 problems but a...

Content:

[name],

If you did not collect the name, use "Hi!" or any other saying that means "hello".

I prefer to deliver upon my promises before anything else ... so as promised, **Click here to download your copy of [lead magnet name]!**

Since you're on this email list, I know that you have a problem with [whatever problem your product/service solves].

You've spent your precious money trying to solve this problem.

Even worse ... you've wasted your time trying to solve this problem.

I know. I've *personally* been there.

And it's terrible.

This link will help solve your problem with [whatever problem your product/service solves]. [link to your sales page]

Don't delay. You know what they say - bad news gets worse with time ... as do problems.

Make it happen,

[your name]

[http://yoursite.com]

Email #2

Timeframe:

- 24 hours after Email #1

Subject lines:

- Argh! It shouldn't be this hard
- Does this bother you too?
- [Symptom of problem]?

Content:

[name].

Are you tired of [symptom of problem]?

You're not alone.

There are thousands of people trying to solve [problem your product/service solves].

People (probably even you) have tried ["Bad" solution to the problem #1], ["Bad" solution to the problem #2], **and even** ["Bad" solution to the problem #3].

Yet, at the end of the day all you really want is [result of your product/service].

You're tired of all the gimmicks promising X, Y, and Z.

I get it.

But, you'll **never** get past this point unless you do something about it ...

Click Here to do something about it. [link to your sales page]

Problem solved,

[your name]

[http://yoursite.com]

Email #3

Timeframe:

- 24 hours after Email #2

Subject lines:

- What's working, right now
- Did you see this?
- This works!
- [Product Name]

Content:

Ok [name],

This is *literally* it.

This product [link to your sales page] is going to solve your problems with [whatever problem your product solves].

It's *that* simple.

And … to be honest, I'm a little astonished you're *still* having this problem.

What [product/service name] does is:

Benefit #1 - blah blah blah - Address "bad" problem #1 if possible *(from email 2)*

Benefit #2 - blah blah blah - Address "bad" problem #2 if possible

Benefit #3 - blah blah blah - Address "bad" problem #3 if possible

Remember! There is a difference between "benefits" and "features". List the <u>BENEFITS</u> to the end user.

- ie. Get more ladies with X
- Get more sales with X
- Don't be alone on X holiday with Y
- etc, etc, etc.
- BENEFITS!!!!

⇒ **Click Here to get more information about [product/service]**

I look forward to working with you and … I'll talk to you later!

[your name]

[http://yoursite.com]

Features-Advantages-Benefits

Email #1

Timeframe:

- Immediately or a couple hours after subscribed (if using concurrent email series)

Subject lines:

- Per your request: [lead magnet]
- Here's your download
- As you requested... [lead magnet]
- You'll be amazed!
- By the numbers
- What is this?

Content:

Hi [name]!

If you did not collect the name, use "Hi!" or any other saying that means "hello".

I deliver upon my promises. **Please Click here to download your copy of [lead magnet name]!**

You know what's really cool?

All the things [product/service name] can do / has / consists of!

Here's a short list ... *and* of course there's a LOT more; however, inboxes can only hold so much ;)

1. [Biggest feature]

2. [2nd biggest feature]

3. [3rd biggest feature]

Remember, features are distinctive attributes or facts. For example,

- Holds 1,000 songs
- 8 hour battery life
- 3.5 hours of video tutorials
- Made with handwoven bamboo
- Made in America

All of these awesome features combined result in a pretty amazing product … if I do say so myself!

Click here to see more awesome features [link to product's sales page]

I'm excited for you!

[your name]

[http://yoursite.com]

Email #2

Timeframe:

- 24 hours after Email #1

Subject lines:

- Why we win
- Round 3. FIGHT!
- Tell us, what's easier?

Content:

[name].

Real talk.

We have some competition when it comes to [product/service name].

Competition is good. It breeds creativity and ... most importantly ... better results for you!

Right now, our #1 competitor is [name of #1 competitor].

Note: If you don't have a true "competitor" ... "fight" the status quo or what happens if they don't resolve the problem. For example, if you don't quit smoking, you may get lung cancer and die.

This is why we're better:

1. [Reason #1 why you're better]

2. [Reason #2 why you're better]

3. [Reason #3 why you're better]

For more reasons we're better and to get started, you'll want to ...

Click Here for more reasons why we have what you need! [link to sales page]

Whew, what a fight!

[your name]

[http://yoursite.com]

Email #3

Timeframe:

- 24 hours after Email #2

Subject lines:

- Achievement Unlocked!
- This is the shortcut
- 3 ways to [solve whatever problem your product/service solves]

Content:

[name]!!

I know exactly what you've been waiting for ... a *precise* list of "what we're going to do for you."

So, here it is:

1. Benefit #1

2. Benefit #2

3. Benefit #3

Remember! There is a difference between "benefits" and "features". List the <u>BENEFITS</u> to the end user.

- ie. Get more ladies with X
- Get more sales with X
- Don't be alone on X holiday with Y
- Never worry about your battery dying during the day
- Every time you wear a bamboo dress, you're saving a tree!
- etc, etc, etc.
- BENEFITS!!!!

⇒ **Click Here to get more information about [product/service]** [link to your sales page]

I look forward to working with you and ... I'll talk to you later!

[your name]

[http://yoursite.com]

ANNEX B: How To Figure Out What To Sell (Value Ladder Concept)

This is a blog post from https://www.crazyeyemarketing.com/blog/how-to-create-a-value-ladder-for-your-sales-funnel/. I think it will be incredibly helpful for those that are struggling to figure out what to try to sell with regard to up-sells, down-sells, and cross-sells.

How To Create A Value Ladder For Your Sales Funnel

This Is Important!

Before charging head first into sales funnel creation, you **_need_** to take the time to map out your value ladder – your products and services mapped in ascending order of value and price.

The Value Ladder

General Concept

As people "ascend" your value ladder, they're offered more value; however, this value comes at a price ($).

Note: Value doesn't necessarily mean "more". You can also provide greater value by saving people time.

Tiers

Your value ladder doesn't necessarily need 5 tiers as shown in the diagram above. Offering multiple value tiers at various price points gives you more opportunity to give your customers exactly what they need.

Lead Magnet

The freebies you give away to grow your list(s) and get people in the door.

- **Price:** Free
- **Goals:** Qualify & Capture Leads
- **Examples:** Checklist, Guide, Video, Free Sample, Trial, Coupon

Initial Offer

The low-end products you offer that ideally cover the cost of advertising and "prove" the lead has enough "pain" that they're willing to spend money to resolve it. Many times you'll see "Free plus Shipping" offers.

- **Price:** < $10
- **Goals:** Re-Capture Ad Spend & Qualify Customers
- **Examples:** Book, Course, Product

1st Tier

The low-mid range products and services you offer generate profit while simultaneously building customer's trust as they receive more value from you and your business.

- **Price:** < $100
- **Goals:** Increase Profits & Build Trust
- **Examples:** Course, Productized Service, Product

2nd Tier

The high-mid range products and services you offer generate profit, ideally recurring revenue, from membership and continuity programs.

- **Price:** < $1,000
- **Goals:** Increase Profits & Recurring
- **Examples:** Course, Membership, Custom Service, Product

Top Tier

The biggest and best product/service you have!

- **Price:** > $1,000
- **Goals:** Increase Profits & Recurring
- **Examples:** Done For You Service, Masterminds

Product Based Businesses

I know what you're thinking, "A value ladder sounds nice, especially for digital and service-based businesses, but I sell physical products and things just aren't "fitting"."

Don't worry, I've got you covered!

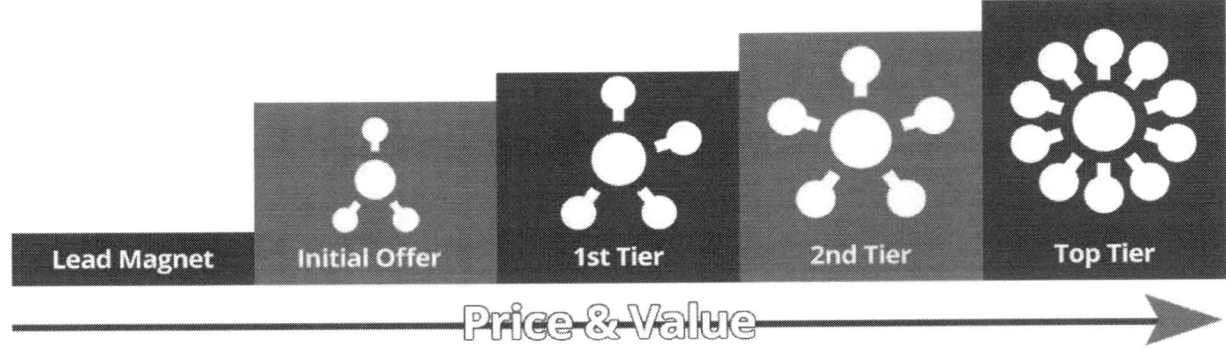

Incorporate The Hub And Spoke Model

The "hub" is the core product and the "spokes" are all the accessories and peripherals that "enhance" the core product.

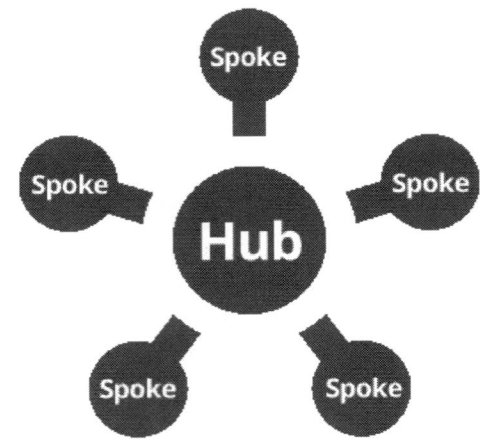

Many times, businesses that sell physical products can't "ascend" customers the same way digital and service-based businesses can.

For example, if you sell cars, you can develop and give away a lead magnet and you can likely come up with an initial offer for under $10 (ie. a car buying guide). However, after those first two steps ... there's not much ... you gotta sell a car!

You're not going to try and sell a motorized bicycle, then a scooter, then a motorcycle, then a car, then a nicer car, then an even nicer car *(at least not in one sitting)*. It simply doesn't work that way; however, after the individual purchases a car, they're going to need a lot more stuff – accessories, maintenance, insurance, credit, etc. for years to come.

The car is the "hub" and the additive products/services are the "spokes".

Eventually, *ideally*, when the individual is ready for a new car, they'll ascend to the next level, get a new car (hub), and start buying more stuff (spokes).

Another Example (Retail)

A few years ago, when I first came across the value ladder concept, I tried to apply it to an ecommerce business that also had a brick & mortar location. This particular retailer sold women's clothing – dresses, to be exact.

They offered many different types of dresses from seasonal, to professional, to formal, to wedding ... what "appeared" to be a natural ladder ... and it was, somewhat.

Many times, women would come in for a seasonal dress and leave with two or more dresses – for work and for play. However, there were many occasions where women would only need one type of dress for one specific occasion – ie. a formal occasion.

This was where the hub and spoke model came into play as there are a TON of accessories with formal wear – shoes, bags, jewelry, makeup, etc.

Let's look at a woman that came in and purchased a formal dress. In this case, a wedding dress, even though it's "technically" the next step in the value ladder, it doesn't have to be the next step ... *especially* if she's not engaged and/or doesn't have a boyfriend *(or girlfriend, whatever floats your boat – not the point)*.

The point is, there are likely many seasons and occasions for more dresses (hubs) and accessories (spokes) between now and then that can be capitalized upon, if done correctly.

If it makes sense to ascend people up your ladder, ascend them. If not, be sure to incorporate enough spokes!

Offer Continuity

Often, customers will not ascend your entire value ladder *ever*, much less in one sitting. For those that do ascend, it can take weeks, months, or even years to ascend to the next level.

This is where offering a continuity program or recurring offer comes into play because it helps **accelerate ascension** while increasing **capitalization**.

For example:

- A car dealership can offer oil changes. Cars need oil changes, making this is a natural offer.
- A dress shop can offer a subscription service where every month or season they send out the appropriate style of sunglasses for maybe $10/mo. Not only will this sell more sunglasses, but it

serves as a reminder to the customer that they need a new dress for the new season!

- Digital products businesses can offer a community and/or premium support as a recurring offer.
- Dentists offer 6 month check-ups.

Bundles & Down-sells

Bundles and down-sells come in handy, especially if you're stuck or are truly limited in what you have to offer.

Let's say you sell 10 different products, that all cost $30, and don't have any additional accessories, even ones you could offer as an affiliate. *(unlikely, but this is a hypothetical!)*

Could you create bundles of these products? Maybe a 3 pack, 5 pack, and 10 pack? There's your ladder!

For example:

- This concept can be applied to businesses that only offer one thing, for example, a soft serve ice cream shop. Beyond up-selling more ice cream, they can offer a punch card for $X that grants the holder 5 cups, 10 cups, 20 cups, etc. at various price breaks.
- Barber shops can also take advantage of the bundling concept. While many offer other services like shaves, dyeing, massages, etc., that can be bundled into packages, they can also bundle visits onto punch cards in a similar fashion to the ice cream shops.
- Here at Crazy Eye Marketing, we offer courses and resources individually and as a bundle we call The Vault (https://www.crazyeyemarketing.com/join/).

Down-Sell Mega Tip!

One of the best ways to help people ascend your value ladder quickly is to reduce the entry price to the next tier.

How?

Payment plans!

Let's say your 1st Tier product costs $97 and your 2nd Tier product costs $247, you can split your 2nd Tier product into 3 easy payments of $93.67!

Doing this makes the 2nd Tier product a no-brainer as it costs less than the 1st Tier product (at least for *today* – which is what the mind tends to focus on [instant gratification]).

Reverse The Entire Ladder!

This entire time I've been talking about having customers *ascend* your value ladder, but what if you reversed it and had them *descend?!*

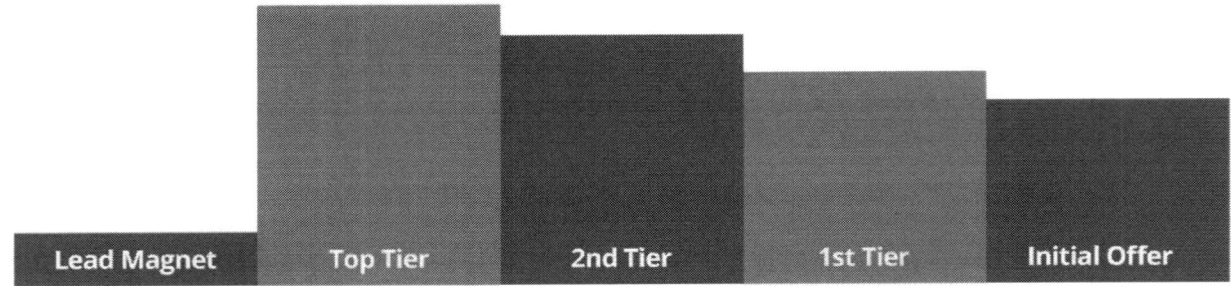

You still start with a lead magnet in order to attract and qualify leads, but then you'll go straight into presenting your top tier offer!

If they're not interested, try a "down-sell mega tip" (payment plan). If that doesn't work, move to the 2nd Tier offer. If that doesn't work, try a payment plan. If that doesn't work, move to the 1st Tier offer, and so on.

Who knows, maybe implementing a reverse value ladder will yield greater results... it's certainly worth trying!

Annex C: How To Quickly "Create" Content

After having read this book, it's easy to see you are going to need quite a bit of content for your funnel to be successful.

You need Main Series content to help you gauge interest.

You need Micro Sales Funnel content to help you sell your products and services.

You need content that looks good in various mediums (web pages, email, advertisements, Facebook Messenger, phone calls, text messages, direct mail, etc.)

It's a lot.

The good news is, there's already more content on the Internet than anyone knows what to do with and you're actually able to repurpose that content!

For instance, you can embed YouTube videos on your website. Simply create a page, embed the video, add a few bullets to relate the video to your audience and then to your business, and boom! You have a piece of content!

You can also use tools like sniply (http://snip.ly/) to inject a call-to-action on a website you don't even own. For example, here's a sniply CTA injected on and article that's posted on Entreprenuer.com:

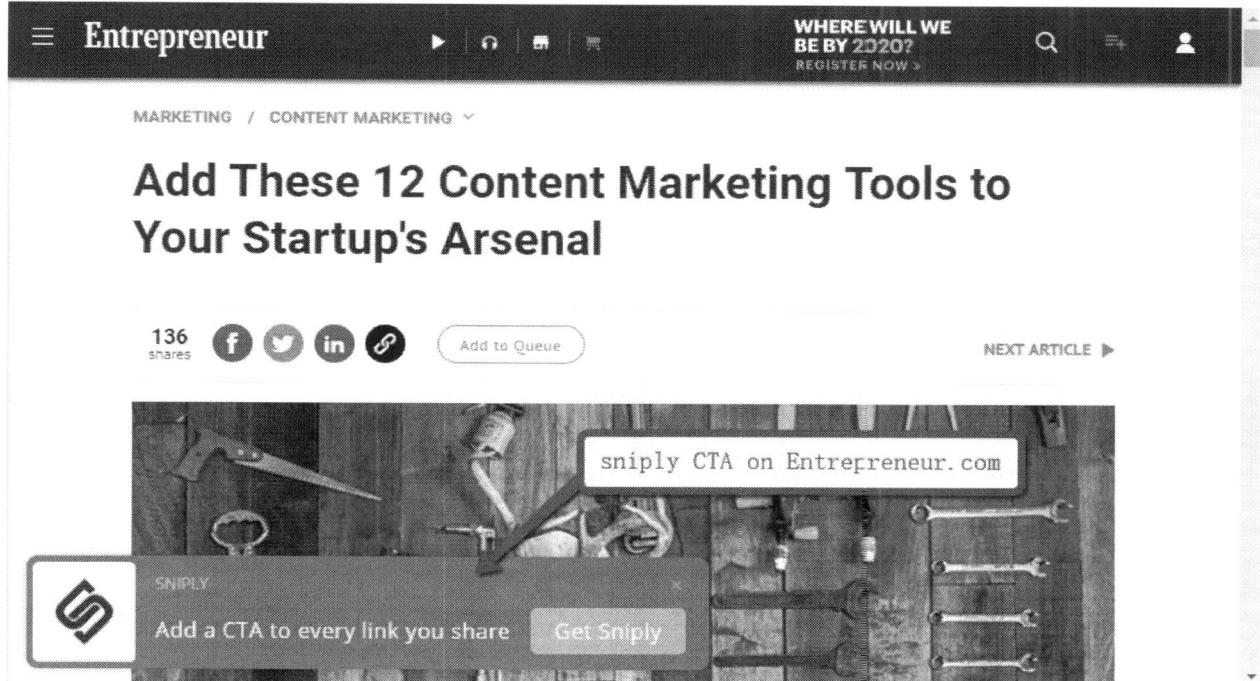

Pretty cool, right?!

You can use these CTAs to bring people back to your website, Micro Sales Funnels, and offers.

That's it for this section.

I just wanted to point out that even though it's best to have all of your own content, it's not always possible or practical and it's best just to get something in place first.

By using curated content, you'll be able to launch your Interest Driven Sales Funnel even faster!

Printed in Great Britain
by Amazon